WOMANHOURS

WOMANHOURS

A 21-Day Time Management Plan That Works

GRETCHEN HIRSCH

St. Martin's Press · New York

Library of Congress Cataloging in Publication Data

Hirsch, Gretchen.
    Womanhours: a 21-day time management plan that works

    1. Woman—Time management.   I. Title.
HQ1221.H57   1983   640'.43   83-10892
ISBN 0-312-88709-4
ISBN 0-312-88710-8 (pbk.)

Design by Mina Greenstein

First Edition
10 9 8 7 6 5 4 3 2 1

This book is dedicated to the memory
of two special men,

my father, WYNNE M. SILBERNAGEL, M.D.,

and my friend, MILTON M. PARKER, M.D., PH.D.

Contents

Acknowledgments   *ix*

Preface   *xi*

Section 1: DAYS 1–8
in which you discover why you're
in the mess you're in

DAY 1   Are You an Ideal Woman?   3

DAY 2   The Time Log to End All Time Logs   *11*

DAY 3   "What Did You Do All Day, Dear?"   *16*

DAY 4   You're an Executive, Starting Today   *24*

DAY 5   "What Do You People Want from Me, Anyway?"   *30*

DAY 6   A Mission Is Not Just a Spanish Church   *34*

DAY 7   Good Goals and Obtainable Objectives   *39*

DAY 8   Positive Planning   *44*

Section 2: DAYS 9–14
in which you discover new ways
to solve old problems

DAY 9 The Fearsome Five: Typical Time Management
        Foul-ups   51
DAY 10 The Fritters and the Fritterers   58
DAY 11 Delegation: Dumpers, Saints, and Managers   67
DAY 12 Pareto's Principle and the Perils of
        Pauline's Procrastination   72
DAY 13 Fatigue: The Woman's Companion   80
DAY 14 The Old Frazzle-Dazzle   86

Section 3: DAYS 15–21
in which you discover that the first
two sections didn't have all the answers

DAY 15 More Help for the Fritters   95
DAY 16 Dandy Delegation: Part 2   103
DAY 17 Finishing Off Filling In   111
DAY 18 Some More Rest for the Weary   118
DAY 19 Your Last Fracas with Frazzle   123
DAY 20 Hard Questions   128
DAY 21 The Last Gasp and a New Start   134

Suggested Reading   137
Index   139

Acknowledgments

Writing is a solitary occupation, and a writer needs a network of people to talk to, touch, and count on. The following people were my network, and I'd like to say thanks:

to Nancy Taylor, Penny Lauer, Jane Hadley, Ellen Frey, Judy Parrish, Carol Luper, Joyce Reiber, and Pat Barton for their cooperation in the early stages of the project

to Dick Taylor, Winkie Chalfant, Page Cuddy, Linda Koegel, Paul and Percy Jenks, Peggy Calestro, Sue Pidcock, Sheila Keyes, Betty Hirsch, and my friends at Hospice of Columbus and Wednesday morning Bible study for their encouragement at critical times

to Ed Chalfant and Barry Beisner for their good conversation and shaping influence

to MarSue Birtler for her early editorial comment

to my agent, Lynn Seligman, for her professionalism, honesty, and warmth, and to her assistant, Amy J. Browne, for her insight

to my mother, Jane Silbernagel, and my sister, Evie Mc-
Cord, for liking what I wrote

to my son, Stew, and daughter, Tobey, for putting up with
a lot

and especially to Tony, for all the reasons he knows.

Preface

I was born, reared, and will probably die in Columbus, Ohio. I was educated at Denison University and graduated cum laude, Phi Beta Kappa from the Ohio State University in 1965. My husband and I were married in 1963, while I was a junior in college. Our son, Stew, was born six months after my graduation in 1965, and our daughter, Tobey, followed eighteen months later.

We moved to a house in the suburbs (a suburb so preppy it even made the handbook), where we lived happily with our dog, cat, and station wagon. ("See Spot run!") As a "young matron," I spent the years just as all my friends did—taking care of kids and doing enormous amounts of volunteer work. My affiliations included the Junior League of Columbus (Project Development Chairperson, Rape Task Force Chairperson, Hospice Task Force Chairperson, Education Coordinator, trainer), Childhood League, Inc. (this organization runs a center for developmentally delayed preschool children; I served as Chairperson of Public Relations, Fundraising Business Manager, and General

Treasurer, as well as dancing, singing, and doing stand-up comedy for the annual fund-raiser, which makes thousands of dollars each year), St. Mark's Episcopal Church (Member of the Vestry, Commission Chairperson, Vacation Bible School Superintendent, Delegate to Diocesan convention), Telemom Hot Line (midnight to 4 A.M. shift; nobody else would take it), Symphony Club (Program Chairperson, Vice-President), Hospice of Columbus (Bereavement Study Group, Board member, Chairperson for Finance, and Chairperson of the Board) and others. Meanwhile, I also took continuing education classes, worked part-time as a physician's office assistant, and served as a teacher's aide.

At age 33, it all caught up with me, and I went into the hospital with the ailments described in the first chapter of *WOMANHOURS*. This experience frightened me enough to make me take a year off and survey some options about how I would live the rest of my life. It was out of this searching that my business, also called *WOMANHOURS*, was born. I reasoned that anyone who could exhaust herself so completely had to know something about time management, even if it was only how not to do it. So, drawing on my own experience, the tales I heard from other women, my volunteer and continuing education training, and a great deal of independent research, I opened *WOMANHOURS*. My husband, who really does believe in equality, but not in housework, capitalized the venture, and I held my first classes in 1978.

Since then I've changed considerably. The outer shell is still the same—button-down shirt, Shetland sweater, sensible skirt, and all. Underneath, however, a new identity has emerged, not that of Superwoman, but that of My-own-woman. I even have a title now. I'm a time management specialist, a woman other women, companies, associations, and groups pay to help them sort out their time management dilemmas.

Through it all, I've continued to live in the suburbs with the original husband (personal growth doesn't have to equal divorce), the kids, the dog, a new cat, and the station wagon with the genuine imitation wood-grain panels. Today, though, life is very different, very new, and very rewarding. I've found the balance, and so can you.

GRETCHEN HIRSCH
March 1983

DAYS 1-8

in which you discover why you're in the mess you're in

DAY 1

Are You an Ideal Woman?

Different voices, different women.

> "I'd like to get more organized and eliminate some stress and guilt from my life."—Diana, 42, secretary, married, two children

> "I want to learn how to get people to help me, so I'm not always doing everything and feeling angry—and then feeling guilty for being mad."—Bonnie, 28, housewife, three children

> "I want to handle the things I must and have time to do the things I enjoy."—Pat, 35, program director, divorced, two children

> "I want to stop letting insignificant things clutter up my life, so that I can have time to do the things I want to do."—Harriet, 50, secretary, grown children

> "I want to find the time to have some fun."—Sally, 36, saleswoman, head of household, one young child

"I'd like to change the kind of volunteering I'm doing. I have only a little time, and I'd like it to count. How do I say no to friends, particularly newly employed friends, who want reliable old Carol to do the same old things, and take on their commitments as well?"—Carol, 37, housewife, seven children

Different voices, different women, but sisters under the skin. No matter how dissimilar these women are from one another, they share a common concern. Because they think they don't have enough time—for work, for fun, for enrichment—they feel overstressed, anxious, and guilty.

But they're just misinformed. They have the time they need to do the things they want; they simply don't know how to structure that time.

It isn't that they haven't tried. They've read articles and books on time management. They make schedules and lists; they rank their priorities; their calendars (the one on the desk, the one on the wall, and the one in the briefcase) are organized and current. They give every appearance of good self-management. The fact is, those long "to-do" lists and split-second schedules are dead giveaways that they've lost control of their time. All these women are at the mercy of the clock and at least a half-dozen other people. In this respect, though they are disparate types, they are representative of women as a group. They are the kinds of women who've been my clients, and until a few years ago, I was one of them, too.

Several years ago, a gaggle of doctors stood around my hospital bed, scratching their heads, saying they didn't know what was wrong with me. I had a rash, so they tested me for lupus. I had afternoon fevers; maybe it was TB. I had a heart murmur; that suggested rheumatic heart disease. I cried a lot. Could I be depressed? None of the symptoms made sense, and all the sophisticated tests were coming back negative. Though finally they discovered a minor viral infection, it was not the kind of thing that usually lands people in the hospital. What else was going on? The "what else" was too many people, not enough time. Too much responsibility. Not enough help. Too many needs. Not enough resources. Too much everything, and not enough me. I was a wife, a mother, a part-time employee, a part-time student, a full-time community volunteer—and a mess.

I'm sometimes a slow learner, so as soon as I was released, symptom-free, I jumped back onto the treadmill—and the fever returned.

At that point serendipity took a hand. My doctor curtailed almost all my activities, and a friend dragged me to a management workshop. I fell in love with the idea of managing, particularly managing my own life, and even more particularly with controlling my time use. I began to read and research, everything from the American Management Association to Heloise's hints, and over the years I developed a time management system tailor-made to my personal requirements.

The system worked so well that I wanted to share it with other women. So my consulting company, WOMANHOURS, was born, the creation not of an expert, but of a woman who's been there, has some common sense, and understands women's special needs.

In time management, as in other areas of life, men and women are different. When a man finds himself swamped, he can often regain his balance relatively easily. He adjusts his schedule, makes a priority list, and has his secretary hold his calls. Tinkering with the machinery of his day, he becomes more efficient.

Women's time problems are not so easily resolved. Most women don't *have* secretaries; they *are* secretaries. And most women are already pretty efficient. Years of meeting the 7:00 A.M., 12:00 M., 6:00 P.M. meal deadline, the 3:00 P.M. school dismissal, the four-hour infant schedule, the Monday washing, the Thursday marketing, and a myriad of other details have forced women into efficiency.

A woman's struggles with time, then, are unlikely to deal with practicalities, although trouble with organizing daily minutiae may be the presenting symptom. Investigating further, however, I find that her difficulties involve not how she uses her time, but how she feels about it. Nine times out of ten, how she feels is guilty.

People feel guilty when they fail to measure up to standards of performance that have been dictated by law or custom as being acceptable. In the Bad Old Days, there were strict rules about women's comportment and function. They were to keep the home fires burning, beat the clothes on the rock better than the lady in the next cave, learn 1,001 simple ways to fix mastodon meat, produce and rear little cavepersons, and die. Glamorous it wasn't, but it was secure. Cavewomen probably groused about the workload, but they accepted their destiny. They were burdened down with firewood, not guilt. If, by chance, a woman did stray from the code of conduct, there was always someone around with a club to remind her of her duty.

The trouble with the Good New Days is that, because nobody can agree on the rules anymore, more women feel guilty more of the time. Today, there are at least two standards of behavior governing any life choice a woman can make. Much of the time these standards are diametrically opposed, and the role models that represent the opposing sides are constantly in flux. Colette Dowling tells us that we all have a "Cinderella Complex." Women's collectives respond that "Sisterhood is Powerful." Anita Bryant discovers that homosexuals are just plain folks and gets divorced. "Free to Be" Marlo Thomas gets married. Housewife Phyllis Schlafly testifies about sexual harassment in the workplace, while activist Jane Fonda produces a light, amusing movie about it. You can't tell the players without a scorecard anymore.

Exhilarated by all their new options, women are nonetheless aghast to discover that the privilege of making choices has a stinger in the tail. In choosing one alternative over the other, they can no longer simply conform to a single common standard of behavior. They can't accommodate everyone anymore. Their choices will not win universal applause. Since they can't find comfortable norms, since every choice they make is somehow wrong, women exhibit degrees of guilt ranging from near-immobilization to a mild indecisiveness. No longer do their men have to bop them on the bean. Armed with society's club, they do the job on themselves.

For example: Suppose a young woman chooses to stay at home with her family. One faction will give her a standing ovation, but others will denounce her. She's wasting her creativity. Her brain will turn to Post Toasties. Her children will be warped by "smother love." So, out to work she goes. *Ms.* Magazine will propose a toast to her determination, but another chorus will shriek that she shouldn't be working. Her kids will all grow up to push dope; they will shrivel from lack of "lovin' from the oven." Her husband, threatened by her independence, will leave her.

Or suppose an under-thirty-year-old woman is unmarried. She might like it, but her mother doesn't. What's the matter with her, anyway? Can't she find some nice young man? (No.)

Time passes, and now the unmarried woman is over thirty. She may think she's fulfilled in her work and her relationships, but what does she know? Society tells her that underneath that contented veneer, she's really a pariah—a calculating, castrating career woman, who probably has sexual-orientation problems.

What about the married woman who chooses not to exercise her reproductive capability? Some call her childfree and envy her. Others call her childless and pity her—vociferously, and in public.

It's no trick at all to make women feel guilty about their life decisions, because no matter what their age, status, or occupation, most women share a deeply inculcated belief, a vague, undefined sense, that whatever else she may do with her life, a woman's "real career" should be to respond to the needs of everybody else. Society's message is still very clear. The "ideal woman" is a servant, a functionary who smooths, soothes, and pats life into shape for her husband, children, relatives, boss, coworkers, friends, and community institutions. She is always serene and calm. Of course, many of the situations to which she must respond today are complex, so while she must never lose her basic passivity, she must at the same time be quick-witted, strong, and resourceful. She should, in short, combine all the best attributes of Betty Friedan, Raquel Welch, Nancy Drew, and the Virgin Mary.

Most women, to a greater or lesser extent, buy into this schizophrenic model of ideal womanhood. Employed or housewives, they juggle their way through life, doing the best they can to gratify all their "significant others." Now and then, they manage to keep all the balls in the air. Much of the time, though, they feel inept. And guilty—always guilty.

Women's guilt sounds something like this:

"I have a job, a husband, kids, and a house. I'm doing okay at work, but I don't do enough with my kids." Or:

"Everything's all right at home, but I don't do enough at the office to advance as fast as I'd like." Or:

"I'm really balancing all the work well, but I don't do enough of the things I'd like to."

All these women, already overachievers, feel guilty because for some reason they believe there is more they can and should do each day. If we decode their messages, however, what they're really saying is, "I have too much to do and not enough time to do it. I'm not meeting my standards; I'm failing; I'm guilty."

Guilt-ridden women often see time management as a way out of a no-win situation. If they only had a little more time— just a couple more hours a day—they could make everybody happy again. They could give more "quality time" to their husbands and kids. Or join the task force on juvenile justice. Or finish the laundry once. Or get the promotion. Or take Underwater Calculus 402.

Such speculations are false. More hours in the day would simply reinforce Parkinson's Law. (Work expands to fill the time available for it.) Too, time management, as customarily taught (usually by men), doesn't get to the heart of women's dilemmas. Offering time-saving tips to women is like slapping more chrome on a car that gets five miles per gallon. It looks pretty; it sells the product, but it doesn't solve the transportation problem.

Women need a different kind of time management help. Instead of a system that shows them how to cram more and more tasks into less and less time, women need a system that will allow them to respond to those people whose needs they choose to meet, but free them from the delusion that they can be all things to all people. Their system should set them up as executives in charge of their own lives.

In *The Effective Executive,* Peter Drucker defines executives as "those who are expected . . . to make decisions in the normal course of their work that have significant impact on the performance and results of the whole." That definition certainly includes every woman I know. Yet most women don't act like executives; they act like junior subordinates in charge of feather unruffling. People-pleasers, they squander their time in an endless round of approval-seeking, both on the job and at home. They don't need time-saving tips, they need reorientation.

This book is about reorientation. I think that the WOMAN-HOURS system can give you the structure you need to manage your life and time. You can learn to do your work and still find the time to be a friend, a lover, a partner—to do all the things that make women's lives rich and fulfilling.

The WOMANHOURS system is designed to take twenty-one days to learn. There's a simple reason. Behaviorists tell us that it takes three weeks of doing something every day to make it a habit. Don't cheat yourself out of the money you spent to buy this book by hustling through it. Take your time. Do the exercises. Form the habit—a habit that can make your life more fun.

EXERCISE 1: Are You an Ideal Woman?

Below, take no more than two to three minutes to list, by name, every person whose needs you have met in the last six months. Usually family and friends are the first on the list, but don't forget co-workers, the Sunday School class, the carpool. When you have finished, count the names on your list. Now, STOP READING UNTIL YOU HAVE COMPLETED YOUR LIST.

How many names do you have listed? The average that is quickly recalled is twenty to forty. Is your list shorter? Longer? Why? Where on your list did you include your own name? You didn't? Why not? Read the instructions again. Are you not a person? Did including yourself simply not occur to you? Why not? If you did put yourself on the list, were you last? Why or why not? Think about it until tomorrow.

DAY 2

The Time Log to End All Time Logs

Just as a doctor needs to discover what's making you sick before he or she can prescribe a remedy, you need to know exactly what you do with your days before you can cure your time management ills. There's only one way to find out, and that's keeping a time log. Because the one you'll be using is so detailed, it's called the "time log to end all time logs." After you've worked with it for a week, you'll know not only how you spend your time, but also how efficiently you function, how your daily rhythm fluctuates, and how you feel about what you do.

It is one thing to give lip service to your value structure; it is quite another thing to live it out. The time log will demonstrate whether your words and actions are congruent. No matter what you may say about what you prize, the fact is that how you spend your time is how you live your life.

Women who live in tune with their priorities invariably produce time logs that reflect their confidence in their choices. There is a certain predictability and rhythm in their time use. This is not to say that they don't have crises and bad days. They

too have washers that throw up at 10:00 P.M. and children who
do the same the first thing in the morning. They have flat tires
and fights with their husbands. But no matter what inconveniences arise, their days manage to stay on track. At least some
uninterrupted portion of each day is spent in planned, high-
priority activities.

On the other hand, women embroiled in a values conflict
turn out fragmented time logs. There are an inordinate number
of hours spent shifting from task to task, and a much greater
percentage of low-priority busy work being ground out each
day. Their logs point out an inability to focus on single issues,
and a loss of life direction.

These symptoms need not be fatal. Acting on one's priorities
is not a gift, but a skill, and it can be learned.

To make the learning easier, a sample copy of the time log to
end all time logs is included at the end of this chapter. You'll
need a spiral-bound notebook to make your own set of sheets.
Make your entries beginning today and continuing through Day
8. As you read Section 2, you'll get a respite from record keeping, but when you arrive at Section 3, you'll pick up the time log
habit again. Once you've absorbed the WOMANHOURS principles and techniques, you'll see a marked difference between the
first set of records and the second.

The time log should be carried with you as you go about your
daily routine (or nonroutine), and your entries made continually. *Don't* try to remember everything and record it all at
night. Memory is too undependable. (Quick, what did your
child wear to school this morning?) Data collected this way are
unreliable, so if you forget your log for more than an hour, pick it
up where you are.

To begin, enter your activity in column 1. Be precise. Was
that phone call for business or was it personal? How about
breakfast? Did you prepare it just for yourself or for your entire
family? Did you fix different things for different people? Did
your preparation also include cleanup? At work, did you interrupt your work to answer questions? Whose? Who dropped by

the office? Include details. Sex, violence, coffee breaks, waiting time—write it all down.

Columns 2 and 3 are both headed "Time." In column 2, enter the time you begin each activity, starting with getting out of bed in the morning and ending when you pull your feet into the sack at night. Let's see how long your days actually are. (And your nights. If you're the mother of an infant or small child, some days really are twenty-four hours long!) Column 3 is for noting how many minutes the task required. For example, column 1 might read: got up, took shower, got dressed, ran last pair of stockings, had to change outfit. Column 3 would then indicate that this nightmare took forty-five minutes. Or column 1 says: 9:00 A.M., phone call to XYZ Company, on hold, VP not in yet, on hold for her assistant, talk to assistant. Column 3 would show that this exchange took twelve minutes.

Column 4 is the most significant area of the log. It's the spot you rank your activities in priority order. Enter a number from 1 to 4 indicating your assessment of this job's priority (1 = absolutely must do today, 2 = must do, but maybe not today, 3 = routine task, 4 = why am I *doing* this?). During the week you'll be startled by how many important things are assigned a low priority and how many routine tasks suddenly become priority 1 emergencies.

Column 5 deals with your ability to use your own natural rhythm effectively. In column 5, enter H if your energy level is high, L if it's low, and N if you're in neutral, sort of cruising on automatic pilot. As you complete these entries, do you find a consistently good match between columns 4 and 5—between the importance of your duties and your energy and creativity levels? Do you busy yourself with your most important work when you're at peak? Or do you somehow find yourself returning phone calls, eating lunch, or ironing while you're at your most alert and capable? Conversely, do you study your hardest subject or try to master a new skill when you're at your lowest ebb? Do you work with or against your bodily signals?

Column 6 gives you an opportunity to share feelings with

yourself. Jot down a feeling word or phrase about each obligation. Are you bored, excited, tense, comatose? What percent of your day do you spend feeling lousy? How often are you really happy doing what you do? If you spend a lot of time down in the dumps, column 6 may show you why.

The results of your daily logs will surprise you, because your off-the-cuff assessment of your time use is probably quite wide of the mark. Since no one needs to see this log but you, please tell the truth about your activities. You can't learn anything about yourself if you're omitting things you feel "funny" about doing or think are not "important" enough to include. Don't worry about making yourself look good. Only absolute honesty can help you see where you're going.

Maintaining this log is a discipline. (That's the nicest word I can think of for it.) Keep at it, even if for the first couple of days you feel enslaved. By making your entries faithfully, you're beginning to liberate yourself from the clutches of the clock.

EXERCISE 2.

Obviously, this day's exercise is to begin your log. Continue through Day 8.

Sample Time Log

1	2	3	4	5	6
Activity	Time	Time	Priority	Energy	Feeling
	(When I began activity)	(Minutes activity took)			

DAY 3

"What Did You Do All Day, Dear?"

Yesterday you were introduced to your personal time log, and today you're getting comfortable with it. Useful as such a tool is, it can't give you a complete picture of your occupations over time unless you work with it for several months. Nor does it provide a sense of the multiplicity of roles you assume over a period of time.

The task inventory that follows—and that is your exercise for today—fills in the gaps in your self-knowledge. When completed, it furnishes a vivid visual record not only about the work you do but also about the roles you take on while performing your duties.

Role confusion is one of the major causes of time mismanagement. The "What Did You Do All Day, Dear?" inventory, while tedious to fill out, provides eye-popping information concerning your various roles.

You'll notice that the inventory has six columns. Begin by placing a check mark in column 1 beside each task identified in column 2 that you perform at any time—daily, weekly, or periodically.

How do you see yourself? Anytime you perform a task, you are functioning not only as yourself, but also in a role. You are not only Sally Smith but also Sally Smith, wife, or Sally Smith, home manager, or Sally Smith, employed woman. In what roles do you spend the majority of your time? For example, when you pay household bills, are you acting as a wife or home manager? When you sew clothing, is that primarily a creative outlet for you or are you performing a "mother task"? When you decorate your house, do you see that as a wifely duty, a home manager's occupation, or an expression of self?

There are no right or wrong answers. Different women see their tasks from different perspectives. Column 3 will pinpoint your particular position. In this column, assign each task a letter corresponding to the role you're filling when you carry out the assignment: Wife (W), Mother (M), Home Manager (HM), Employed Woman (EW), Volunteer (V), Family Member—daughter, sister, grandmother, niece, etc. (FM), Friend (F), Student (ST), Creative Woman (CW), Myself (MY), Other (O). Don't analyze this too closely, agonizing over each choice. For those tasks in which you feel you are acting in several different capacities, pick the role that predominates. Work quickly; your first instinct is probably correct.

Column 4 asks you to estimate how much time you spend each week on various tasks. This is most easily expressed in decimals (e.g., pay bills—.5 hrs., shop for groceries—1.5 hrs.). If a job is seasonal or occasional, indicate how long it takes, followed by the letter O or S. Should you not wish to determine your time use so precisely, it's sufficient to note simply that a chore is a High (H) or Low (L) time occupation, adding an S or an O appropriately.

In column 5, assess your satisfaction with the tasks you perform. For each one, place an H (for high satisfaction), L (for low satisfaction), or N (for those tasks you neither like nor dislike, but just crank out every day) in the appropriate square.

For the answer to column 6, determine who chiefly benefits from your labors, and assign an S (for self) or an O (for others). Naturally, cooking, cleaning, and other services are tasks you'd do for yourself if you lived alone, but if you're doing those duties for six people—or even for two—the chief beneficiary is someone else.

You can gain a multitude of insights concerning your time management style by glancing over your inventory results. How many tasks do you do? Most women carry out almost all the home chores, and if they are employed, all the job-related tasks are added to the list. Many of my clients are astounded—and rightly so—by the sheer volume of work they do.

Is there a correlation between high time use and high satisfaction? How many of your tasks give you satisfaction, and what percentage of your time is spent carrying out these satisfying responsibilities? Conversely, how many hours are given over to routines you hate?

How much of what you do benefits you? What percentage of your week is taken up in benefits to others? Is the benefit-satisfaction ratio comfortable for you?

To what roles do you devote most of your time? Are you happy about that? What roles would you like to expand? To diminish?

Tomorrow, you'll begin to take control over your roles—and over your life.

EXERCISE 3:

Complete the task inventory. DON'T FORGET TO CONTINUE YOUR TIME LOG.

What Did You Do All Day, Dear?

1	2	3	4	5	6
	Task	Role	Amount of Time	Level of Satisfaction	Beneficiaries
	1. MEALS Prepare list				
	Shop				
	Plan meals				
	Put food away				
	Fix meals				
	Set table				
	Serve meals				
	Clear table				
	Do dishes				
	Bake				
	Preserve food				
	Grow food				
	Prepare garden				
	Plant				
	Weed				
	Other care				
	Harvest				
	Other				
	2. LAUNDRY Gather and sort				
	Wash and dry				
	Pretreat; spot				
	Iron				
	Put away				
	Other				
	3. HOUSEWORK: *light* Vacuum				
	Dust				
	Unclutter				
	Clean baths				
	Change sheets				
	Clean woodwork				
	Make beds				
	Care for plants				
	Empty trash				

1	2	3	4	5	6
	Task	Role	Amount of Time	Level of Satisfaction	Beneficiaries
	Polish silver				
	Other				
	4. HOUSEWORK: *heavy* Wash windows				
	Wash, wax floors				
	Clean basement				
	Clean garage				
	Turn mattresses				
	Care of heavy items				
	Other				
	5. LAWN WORK Mow				
	Weed				
	Fertilize				
	Seed				
	Plant flowers				
	Prepare flowerbeds				
	Other				
	6. CLOTHING Sew buttons, hems				
	Make or alter clothes for self or family				
	Select clothes for family				
	Other				
	7. RECORD KEEPING Pay bills				
	Keep insurance records				
	Keep tax information				
	Keep expense record				
	Keep house information (mortgage, plat)				
	Keep inventory of property				
	Bank accounts				

1	2	3	4	5	6
	Task	Role	Amount of Time	Level of Satisfaction	Beneficiaries
	Stock and bond records				
	Safety deposit box and list of contents				
	Estate planning				
	Keep list of professional advisors current				
	Other				
	8. OTHER WORK Full-time				
	Part-time				
	Volunteer				
	Church				
	School				
	Education for self				
	Other				
	9. CHILD CARE Feed				
	Bathe				
	Dress				
	Pick up after				
	Chauffeur				
	Help with lessons				
	Attend child's activities				
	Health care				
	Just spend time together				
	Recreation with children				
	Teach/Instruct				
	Other				
	10. DECORATOR Choose fabric				
	Choose paint				
	Choose accessories				

Exercise 3 *(Cont.)*

1	2 Task	3 Role	4 Amount of Time	5 Level of Satisfaction	6 Beneficiaries
	Oversee remodeling or decorating				
	Hire tradespeople				
	Other				
	11. HANDYWOMAN Paint				
	Paper				
	Upholster				
	Refinish				
	Make curtains and slipcovers				
	Fix appliances				
	Make home repairs				
	Do major remodeling				
	Other				
	12. CARE FOR FAMILY MEMBERS (other than children), FRIENDS				
	Make hospital, home visits				
	Prepare food				
	Run errands				
	Listening ear				
	Other				
	13. ERRANDS Doctor, dentist				
	Bank				
	Laundry, dry cleaning				
	Pharmacy				
	Post office				
	Other				
	14. RECREATION Crafts				
	Sports				
	Reading				

1	2	3	4	5	6
	Task	Role	Amount of Time	Level of Satisfaction	Beneficiaries
	Friends				
	Family outings				
	Leisure pursuits				
	Other				
	15. OTHER				

DAY 4

You're an Executive, Starting Today

By now, you probably think that all you're going to do for the next three weeks is to fill out forms. Well, relax. Though you do have to keep up with your time log, today's exercise will require more thinking than pencil mechanics. Today you'll begin the process of restructuring your time.

Any time management system is designed to help the client maximize the time spent in pursuits that are satisfying to her and produce desired life results. It is not the time management teacher's job to decide what those results should be. No system should have a bias regarding the relative merit of a client's wishes for her time. Occasionally, a woman will say to me, "Oh, but what I want to do seems so trivial." If it's important to you, it isn't trivial, and no one (including consultants with fancy titles) has the right to disparage it.

One of the biggest names in time management claims that he skims books only for ideas and never reads newspapers or magazines. He seems to think such occupations are insignificant.

That's okay with me, but just because he's an "expert," I don't have to buy his whole package. Near the top of my personal pleasure poll is checking into the easy chair with my mohair blanket and *Harper's Bazaar* or the poems of Wallace Stevens or T. S. Eliot. I'm going to keep right on doing it, too. I take my wants—even the "nonproductive" ones—seriously. And so should you. Don't apologize for your heart's desires, no matter how frivolous they may seem. They're part of what makes you unique. Rather than be embarrassed by their "unworthiness," take action to make time for them.

Frank Bunker Gilbreth, one of America's best-known efficiency experts (though he was more than that), was once asked, "What do you want to save time *for?* What are you going to do with it?" He replied, "For work, if you love that best. For education, for beauty, for art, for pleasure. For mumblety-peg, if that's where your heart lies." I can't improve on that.

What yesterday's task inventory usually shows, however, is that most women are not in a position to choose art, beauty, pleasure, or anything else, because their lives are so mired in the completion of routine tasks. Women's days are taken up with jobs they either actively dislike or simply tolerate because "somebody has to do it." Interestingly, in most cases, the chief beneficiary of these low-satisfaction routines is someone else. Tasks that require long periods of time, provide high satisfaction, and benefit the woman herself constitute only a tiny percentage of the average woman's waking hours.

Many of my clients start fidgeting when we talk about making them the beneficiaries of their own actions. The whole idea makes them edgy. They see benefiting themselves as self-seeking, self-serving, and self-*ish*. They seem to feel that a little enlightened self-interest will transform them into jack-booted Amazons; that seeing to their own needs will make them less kind, less sensitive, less feminine. It's as if they've gone to the doctor with a terrible disease. When the physician produces a vial of wonder drug, the patients beg that it be given to their husbands and children first. But the husbands and children

aren't sick; they're doing just fine, thanks. The cure must begin
with the patient.

Why does the remedy seem so threatening? Though the
women can see the results of the task inventory, though they are
indignant at the injustice of one person shouldering 75 to 90
percent of the load, they'll clap the yoke back on their necks as
fast as I try to lift it. Their reasons for doing so are usually variations on two main themes. They feel bound by culture and tradition or, at the other end of the spectrum, by the women's
movement. The culture and tradition argument goes like this:
"If I start looking out for myself all the time, I'll get to the point
where I don't care about anybody else. I just can't be that cold
and calculating. After all, we're put here on earth to serve others. If everybody just thought about herself, the whole country
would collapse. All this me-first stuff makes me sick."

Me, too. I believe fully that serving and caring for others is a
good thing to do. Nurturing, loving, assisting—all are things
women do well, and all are appropriate roles for women.

But they are also appropriate roles for men. They are *human*
functions for which women have too long assumed almost complete responsibility. Women have an obligation to share the
emotional wealth and to learn to concentrate their efforts in
areas that have meaning for them, rather than trying to right
every social ill single-handedly.

Before I opened WOMANHOURS, I was part of seven community boards in ten years, and the work I did was important. But I
was so busy doing for others that my kids were getting the edge
of my tongue, my husband said I was absolutely no fun anymore, and I never saw my friends. After learning some management techniques through one of the organizations I belonged to,
I realized that *I could choose* which others I wanted to serve; I
didn't have to serve everybody who came down the pike and
asked me. Today I'm part of one community board, one training
organization, one women's network. I help out at my children's
schools on an ad hoc basis and do the same for my church. The

quality and effectiveness of my caring are enhanced, the time I share with others much more valuable. That kind of giving became possible when I started to consider my own needs too. People are a lot like pitchers of water. You can't pour from them forever, without occasionally taking them back to the well. To be able to pour out your concern for others, you simply must show kindness to yourself as well.

Paradoxically, one of the most destructive arguments against enlightened self-care for women comes right out of the women's movement—the popular song argument. You know the one. "I am strong, I am invincible. . . ." Implicit in that lyric is also, "I'm superior, too—a real Wonder Woman." For years, women have been trying to coax their husbands and friends to relinquish the devastating, ulcer-producing myth of Superman. Yet because of our need to prove our capability—our parity with our brothers—we have adopted as our patron saint another cartoon character. She's as phony as he is, and her image makes it doubly difficult to convince women that they need to think about themselves. They're too busy showing the world that they can do it all—perfectly—invincibly.

I'm here to tell you that both men and women are plenty "vincible." Put them under enough stress for a long enough period of time, and they'll both crack. Both men and women need self-care, but it comes more easily to men. And it's essential to good time management.

The WOMANHOURS system will start you down the path to good management by helping you to restructure one role to your advantage. It's much too monumental an undertaking to try to overhaul your entire life at once. Major life changes are made one step at a time, one day at a time. After you've internalized the WOMANHOURS system with one role, it's easy to translate the learning to the next role—and the next—until the life adjustments are made.

Today, then, with the help of your task inventory, you'll choose the role you want to work on. The role you select should be the one that is causing you the most stress. As you glance over the inventory, that role will probably be apparent. It's the one that takes great hunks of time and gives you little satisfaction; it's the role whose tasks are boring, repetitive, or unproductive. It could be home managing or volunteer work or paid employment. It doesn't matter—just make a choice.

Having chosen your problem role, assume an executive position regarding this part of your life. Assuming an executive position doesn't mean that you have to put on a pin-striped suit; it means only that you have to put on an executive mind-set. Make sure the mind-set you put on is that of an *effective* executive.

Ineffectual executives (male and female) and ineffectual women have much in common. They both spend most of their time responding. They involve themselves in far too much detail work; they cope from crisis to crisis. They are late; they are unprepared; they dabble and dither and drive others crazy.

Effective executives, on the other hand, spend their time planning, observing, controlling. Their focus is on results, not procedural details. When faced with change, they ask themselves executive-type questions.

As you go about changing your role, you need to ask questions, too. The three executive questions I recommend are:

1 What results would I like to see?
2 Who else will be affected if I change the way I carry out this role?
3 What am I doing now and what should I be doing?

Today's exercise is to answer Executive Question 1. (Questions 2 and 3 are covered in the next two chapters.) Today, ask yourself, "If I could change the role of (insert yours), what would I like to see happen?" Free your imagination. If you could have things exactly the way you wanted them, how would they be? Maybe you'd like to get more education, or to strike a better balance between work and home, or to have a different kind of relationship with your parents. Whatever it is, unless you have identified and clarified the results you want, no management system can help you.

EXERCISE 4:

In regard to my role of _____, I'd like to see the following results:

CONTINUE THE TIME LOG!

DAY 5

"What Do You People Want from Me, Anyway?"

I already know what you're going to say. Something like, "Big deal! I wrote down everything I'd like to see happen, but I can't change things all by myself. My kids like everything just the way it is. My husband will be a hassle, let alone my boss. I'm not sure it's worth the aggravation."

If you don't know, I can't tell you, but if you've stuck with the reading and record keeping for this long, you're probably pretty highly motivated—and ready for a change.

And you're right. You don't live in a vacuum; others are influenced by your decisions. To produce as little upheaval as possible, you need the answers to Executive Question 2. Who will be affected by my role change? How will they be affected? How can I engage their cooperation in what I want to do?

It's not too hard to figure out who else will be involved and how; the kicker is how to bring them aboard, how to promote cooperation. I advocate a 4-C program.

First, *communicate*. Tell the others what you're trying to do and ask them for their help. You can't generate collaboration among a bunch of people who don't know what you're up to. Clue them in. Let them know what you hope to accomplish. Explain that you want and expect their support.

This kind of assertive communication is difficult for women. We've been conditioned to defer and then to manipulate behind the scenes. That sometimes works, but it's not very rewarding to get what you want by "feminine" chicanery and subtle deception. Now it's cards-on-the-table time. Speak up. Other people can't read your mind, and it's frustrating waiting around for them to try.

Sometimes women will say, "You make it sound so easy! You don't know my husband (or boss or mother). You can't tell him (or her) anything!" That's right, if "telling them something" means making some sort of value judgment about them. Naturally, people tune out that kind of conversation. But I'm not promoting value judgments; I'm pushing "I-message" communication. "You never do anything around here" has a far different ring to it than, "I really get angry when I see five bags of trash in the kitchen." Tell them how *you* feel; don't presume to tell them what *they* think. Strong "I-messages" get results.

Once they know where you stand, *convince* them. Point out that, while things will be different, they will continue to benefit, albeit in different ways. Clarify the positive results of your role change. A more effective employee can help boost productivity and make the bottom line more attractive. A less harried mommy has more time for fun. A wife who's expanding her horizons is far more interesting than a scullery drudge.

Though it's true that achieving your aims will benefit the others too, expect resistance. People don't like change. It makes them uncomfortable. They fight it—often vigorously. Some of these "communicate and convince" sessions can get ugly. After all, we're not talking about the Waltons here; we're talking about normal families and co-workers. Husbands sometimes take these opportunities to inform their stay-at-home wives that since they don't earn the money they don't have any right to bell-yache. Bosses may roadblock by arguing that they "can't make special allowances for you, for God's sake. Then I'd have to do it for everybody!" Children often sense tougher times ahead if you're going to stop pulling the entire load. They may cop out of the whole discussion by remembering an urgent baseball game. They'll "talk to you about it later, Mom. Honest!" Persevere. Realize that all these people feel threatened. They want to know what's *really* behind this odd behavior. The boss wonders if you're going to quit; he or she cringes at the idea of breaking in somebody new. Your husband wonders what's happened to you; have you been hanging out with a bunch of libbers? Your kids just wonder if you've flipped out.

You can defuse their anxiety by moving on to the third C—*consultation*. You've handed these people a lot to chew on. Since they're now the ones with the problem, it's time for you to stop talking and start listening. Really listening. Ask them why they object to your plans, and listen both to what they verbalize and to the unspoken messages. Have them define for you what they think your job is. Ascertain from them what they would most like for you to continue to do and what things they don't consider necessary. Brainstorm your biggest concerns. They may have very inventive solutions that would never have occurred to you.

Then, *compromise*. To compromise doesn't mean that you give up your views in the face of opposition. It means to find those areas on which both sides are in agreement. During the consultation phase, each side probably articulated extreme positions. Now it's time to moderate the extremes, to find the common ground. Accentuate agreement; assist accommodation. The literal meaning of compromise is "to promise together." What aspects of your desired results will the others support? Promise together to work to achieve them.

Your exercise today is to conduct a fact-finding interview with your important others. (Try to pick a time when they are relaxed and receptive.)

EXERCISE 5:

The others affected by my decision are:

Their expectations are:

We agree that:

KEEP YOUR TIME LOG UP TO DATE.

DAY 6

A Mission Is Not Just a Spanish Church

For the past couple of days, you've been involved in an assessment procedure. You've analyzed your present situation and have outlined in general terms the direction in which you'd like to move. All this activity, while essential, has been stage setting; today you'll begin the business of acting out your life change. Today you'll uncover your answer to Question 3, the most important of the executive questions. Your answer will come in the formation of your Mission Statement, the first step of the WOM-ANHOURS system.

To recap, Question 3 asks, "What am I doing? What should I be doing?" This question looks like a cinch. It isn't. While the evidence concerning what you're doing now is all over your task inventory and time log, you have no data concerning what you should be doing.

When women fail at time management, it's here. Stymied at trying to determine what they should be doing, they retreat into efficiency—performing a multitude of tasks and doing them well. But they don't feel gratified. Efficiency doesn't breed happiness; effectiveness does.

As Peter Drucker says, again in *The Effective Executive,* "Efficiency is the ability to do things right. [Effectiveness is] the ability to get the right things done." Doing things right. Doing right things. How different these concepts are from one another, and how sad that so many women are "stuck" with efficiency. To make efficiency the goal of life is to lobotomize women, to transform them from unique, creative human beings into brainless Stepford wives. The waste of womanpower is incalculable. It's a shame and a tragedy.

How do we avoid this misfortune? How do we begin to do our own "right things"?

Much of the time, the experts will tell you that all you need to do is set some goals, work to achieve them, and you'll automatically become more effective. That's sound advice, as far as it goes. All good management systems involve setting goals. There is a problem, however, with women and goal setting. Too often women set their goals according to what they think others require. Their goals may not be what they themselves want, but what they think they *should* want—what they perceive to be socially acceptable norms. This is detrimental in two ways. Societal norms may be antithetical to the women's individual needs, and in almost all cases, these norms are task related.

For example: I am a child of the fifties married to a child of the fifties. We grew up with "Father Knows Best" and "I Love Lucy," and we believed it. So, when in 1976 (the bicentennial of America's independence, as it happened) I opened my own business, change was inevitable, particularly regarding my role as a wife.

It had always been one of my life goals to be a good wife. It remains a goal today. But what is a good wife? If you sit back and wait a few minutes, the culture will sing out the attributes loud and clear. A good wife:

1 cooks like Julia Child;
2 handles all social obligations;
3 keeps her body attractive through rigorous exercise and

the use of every product marketed to enhance feminine allure;

4 keeps her mind active, not for the obtaining of knowledge or wisdom, but to be an interesting conversationalist for her husband;

5 is sexually adept and inventive;

6 is a better counselor than Dr. Joyce Brothers, at no cost or obligation to the counselee;

7 washes and irons, never allowing her husband to appear with a wrinkle or a missing button. If he's a slob, it's her fault.

And on and on. Task piled on task. This kind of task-oriented definition has all the answers. Though it contains enough work for a team of oxen, it's simplistic. Do all the right steps, and you'll be a good wife.

The crunch comes when you miss a couple of steps.

The difficulty with a task-oriented definition is that all the tasks become equally important, and to fail at one or two of them is to blow the whole role. Suppose, as Priscilla Goodwife, you forget that tonight is couples bridge night, you cook an "adventure" dinner that tastes like a trip through a tire factory, you don't get your hair washed, and you "have a headache," all in one day. Four tasks right down the drain. Four things you should have done and didn't. It isn't that you're disorganized, or harried, or human. If you don't do the jobs, you're a failure. And since every day you live, you fill a variety of roles, and each role will contain tasks you don't complete, that's a lot of failure—and a lot of guilt.

Women can begin to control their time—and their guilt—as soon as they absorb the first rule of good time management. That is, that *tasks do not define roles; people do.*

Before you can set goals effectively, you must come to *your own definition* of your role as wife, mother, businesswoman, volunteer—whatever function you've chosen to alter.

To help my clients untangle their societally induced role confusion, I ask them to toss out all of their previously held assumptions about what women should do, and to write a simple statement defining their own idea of the essence of their role. There are two criteria for this statement. It must be positive and it must contain *no tasks*—no carpools, no envelope stuffing, no hospital visits, no "things to do today" at all.

Some women find this exercise almost impossible, because they have great difficulty separating what they do from what they are. Their existence is almost totally bound up in performance. The logical consequence of this self-image is that if they stop *doing*, they stop *being*. It's too horrifying even to think about. So they don't.

In my own case, I had to redefine "good wife." I had to dispense with the list of jobs and get down to the real nature of the role. After numerous revisions, my statement read: "A good wife is a woman who promotes relationship-building with her husband." You'll notice it says nothing about cooking, cleaning, or laundry. It is an unadorned statement of what I believe "wifehood" is. I emphasize that this is *my* statement. Because every woman is unique, every declaration will be unique as well.

In preparing your Mission Statement, engaging in a process called "task stripping" is most helpful. To use this technique, prepare a list of every task that you've been taught falls within the purview of the role you're working on. Starting at the top of the list, ask yourself, "Could I drop this task and still be a good . . .?" Strip out all the jobs you can. Assign them to other categories or eliminate them completely. When you've come to the end of the list, find the relationship among the tasks that remain. Those are, for you, the essential core of your role. Build your Mission Statement around them.

Another way to attack the issue is to visualize yourself as being unable to perform tasks, as a victim of something debilitating (but not serious or painful, of course) that makes it impossible for you to go about your accustomed duties. Would you still be a mother? A friend? A valuable community member? Of course you would, because the role is more than the tasks. Identify the essence of the role; reflect it in your Mission Statement.

Mission Statements are as varied as the women who make them. One businesswoman wrote, "A good businesswoman makes a profit for the company and for herself." Another businesswoman's perspective emphasized the service aspects of her job. There are no correct definitions—only personal ones.

Getting your Mission Statement on paper is massively liberating, because once it's written, you can see immediately what your own "right things" are, and you can tell at once whether the things you've been "doing right" are helpful or even necessary. If your tasks have nothing to do with your mission, you need feel no guilt about letting them go. You will be in charge of deciding how to act out the consequences of your Mission Statement. You will know, almost in the twinkling of an eye, what you should be doing.

EXERCISE 6:

Obviously, today's exercise is to write a Mission Statement for the role you wish to change. Later, you may want to draw them up for all your roles, but for now, concentrate on only one.

A(n) _____ is:

KEEP GOING ON THE TIME LOG.

DAY 7

Good Goals and Obtainable Objectives

Now you can set goals. Now that you know what's paramount in your value structure, you can begin to create a personal management system—a "greenhouse" in which to cultivate your aspirations.

To set a goal means to declare what you intend to do. A goal is broad, far reaching; it doesn't include specifics. It's simply something to shoot for. Sometimes a goal can't ever be achieved, and that's all right.

How effectively you manage day by day is determined not by whether you reach your goals, but by whether you carry out your objectives.

An objective is not a goal. It's the subdivision of a goal that deals with specific details. To be complete, an objective must contain: (1) what you will change, (2) a target date for completion, and (3) a way to determine success. Objectives are always concrete, attainable, and measurable.

For example: Every January 1, millions of people set the

same goal. As they hoist themselves out of their easy chairs after a day of Bowl watching, they murmur, "I've got to get some of this blubber off." That's a goal. Everybody talks about it, but the one who shows up on the beach in June with a figure she doesn't have to stuff into a bikini is the one who fixed an objective in her mind and attained it. Her objective may have been specific in terms of pounds (by June 1, I will have lost fifteen pounds), bikini size (by June 1, I will wear a size three), or tape measurement (by June 1, I will measure 36–24–36). Whatever her standard, she stuck with it and achieved the desired result.

Results are the key. On Day 4, you projected in general terms some results you'd like to see in your life. Forming goals and objectives sharpens your vision of those hoped-for results. It helps you to deemphasize routine tasks and to concentrate on meaningful use of your time. Goals and objectives focus your effort and provide a framework for fulfillment.

To demonstrate how goals and objectives work together, here are some examples my clients have come up with over the years. One said, "My goal is to help my kids grow into independent adults." Laudable, indeed. Global in scope. A broad, comprehensive statement. This meets all the criteria for a goal. Her objective was: "By January 1, to have taught my children to cook three simple meals and to have them in charge of dinner once per week. Successful if the meals are on the table and edible." Bravo! She has announced what will be changed, there is a date for completion and a rather inventive measurement of success. She's right, too. Obviusly, if the meals are inedible, progress toward the goal has been halted. If the kids can't eat what they cook, they become dependent on Big Macs and frozen enchiladas. If they can cook for themselves, they've taken a step toward independence.

Another woman, wanting to return to a profession she'd left to have children, said: "My goal is to advance my career." You can't get a much more all-encompassing statement than that. She narrowed her objective down to: "By December 31 to have taken one course in my chosen field. Successful if I pass." I like this objective because it was the strongest of several she could have chosen. She didn't decide just to enroll in the course; success in enrolling would not advance her career. She didn't decide to do independent study. That would be too hard to document for prospective employers, and her career would stay at a standstill. She elected to take the course and pass it—in her case the most useful option.

A third client was head of worship activities at her church. Her goal was: "To facilitate the spiritual growth of the church members." Words like *facilitate*, *enhance*, and *develop* are big favorites in goal setting, because they're umbrella words that allow for all kinds of activities. The objective selected for this goal was: "By December 31, to have provided three different worship experiences apart from Sunday mornings. Successful if 75 percent of those attending feel the experience was worthwhile for them." This is a good objective, but it does demand that there be some kind of feedback mechanism. Success in this case will be judged by others, so there must be a way to gather their reactions. The data-collecting device may be as simple as standing at the church door after the service and asking the worshipers their opinions, or as elaborate as a questionnaire sent days later. That's up to the group, but something must be provided.

Because a great many time management mistakes occur in setting goals and objectives, these goals and objectives require careful consideration. Since success in time management translates into achieving your objectives, it makes sense to formulate the best ones you can. There are several criteria to assist you in choosing possible objectives.

First, how much risk will this objective entail? What will you have to relinquish in order to make this objective happen? Your marriage? Your best friend? A chairmanship? Gourmet meals? What sacrifices are demanded? Are you willing to make them?

Second, is this objective realistic at this time? Do you presently have the resources of money, energy, and personnel to carry out this plan? Perhaps you'll need to break the objective down further into more achievable segments. Maybe it's advisable to expand your time scheme to take resource-dictated unavoidable delays into consideration.

Third, is the objective you've set the simplest way to get the job done? Look again. Seek other options. Brainstorm. There's no sense knocking yourself out if you don't have to. Do it the lazy woman's way.

Don't set yourself up for failure by erecting too many targets. Thirteen goals and a list of objectives as long as your arm is asking for trouble. And give yourself time. Tomorrow is probably too soon to achieve most objectives.

Most important, realize that objectives are not for all time; they can be altered as circumstances dictate. People change; interests change. Don't box yourself into completing an objective just because it's on a list you've made. If it's no longer appropriate, change it or chuck it. Goals and objectives are tools to assist you. You are in charge of them, not the other way around. They don't have to be perfect—and neither do you.

EXERCISE 7:

Write a minimum of one and a maximum of three goals. Set one or two objectives for each.

Mission Statement (from preceding exercise):

Goal 1:   *Goal 2:*   *Goal 3:*

Objective: Objective: Objective:

Objective: Objective: Objective:

ONLY TWO MORE DAYS OF KEEPING YOUR TIME LOG. (I KNOW IT'S HARD.)

DAY 8

Positive Planning

Setting goals and objectives is the sexy part of a management system. Their very orderliness makes them attractive. Their precision is seductive. Women sometimes get so enchanted with them that they forget to go on with the process. They write down their goals and objectives, look them over for a few days, and wait for results. When nothing happens, they toss the goal sheet into a drawer, and get back to business as usual.

They've forgotten to plan. Goals and objectives, no matter how lovingly or conscientiously formulated, don't make a woman effective. They aren't magic; in fact, without planning, all those pretty goals are useless. Planning makes the wheels go around and sounds the bells and whistles. Planning is easy, too, because a plan is nothing more than the "how" something will be accomplished.

For example: If you, like all those other New Year's re-solvers, goal-set to dump some poundage, and if you set your objective, you must now outline how you'll incorporate weight loss behaviors in your life. Will you walk a mile a day? Or eat only 1,200 calories each day? Perhaps you need to buy a postage scale for the kitchen, or to dig out the old calorie counter. They're all plans; they delineate how you'll lose the weight.

My clients are good planners. The woman who wanted independent children planned to give them one cooking lesson a week. This, of course, entailed other planning—finding simple recipes for meals the family enjoyed, familiarizing the children with cooking terminology, and giving them a crash course in nutrition. One plan invariably leads to another.

Some of the planning done by my returning student was to pick up a copy of the university bulletin for enrollment information, to find a baby-sitter, to earn the money to pay the baby-sitter or to work out a cooperative arrangement, to investigate tuition deferments, and more.

The worship chairwoman planned to research liturgical books for unusual worship services, to have her committee design a questionnaire, to appoint three different co-chairpersons for the three services, etc.

When you take the time to do it, you probably plan as well as these women. There are ways, however, to make even the best-laid plans more productive.

I find that planning is most effectively done by starting at the objective and working backward to today, rather than the other way around. This skill takes a little while to hone, but once learned, it's worth the effort. Backward planning helps you to see problem areas you might otherwise overlook.

Returning to the weight loss example: Suppose your objective is to end up with ten fewer pounds to haul around. This objective in place, you begin your backward planning. To accomplish your objective, you need daily exercise. Before you can exercise you need the proper equipment. Before you can acquire the equipment, you have to determine what equipment is necessary. Before you can decide, you have to choose an exercise regimen. Before you can do that, you have to research various types. So *today* you go to the library. It seems a long way from the library stacks to the stacked bikini; in fact, it's the shortest distance, because this kind of planning eliminates the false starts and haphazard groping that so often attend our efforts.

Of course, this example is greatly oversimplified. Other issues to be resolved include: finding a time for exercise, deciding whether to do toe touches en masse in a class or go it alone, defining what kind of class—aerobic or slimnastics, seeing about child care, if that's necessary, and so on. But no matter how elementary the example, the premise is sound. Work backward from the event, asking, "What do I need to do before I can . . .?" Eventually, you'll arrive at an action you can take today, and any action you can take today strikes a blow at one of the biggest time management bugaboos—procrastination.

Surprisingly, though, one of the most satisfying and productive ways to procrastinate is to wallow around in planning—to plan, replan, and alternate-plan.

Sometimes we need an alternate plan, but keep in mind that alternate planning is costly—always in time and frequently monetarily. If the completion of your objective depends on your plan, you definitely need a plan B to fall back on. Otherwise, forget it.

To illustrate: Several years ago, clients of mine were planning a regional meeting for a large group of health educators and consumers. They had made elaborate arrangements and spent big money to fly in the top man in the field to be their keynote speaker. The meeting was scheduled for late November, a very "iffy" time for weather in our neck of the woods. I asked the group what they would do if the weather (or airline strike or other contingency) prevented the speaker from arriving. They had made no alternate plans—a major oversight in this case, for the success of the entire meeting was predicated on the expert's appearing. Alternate planning was a step they should not have omitted.

Ironically, this same group had made elaborate backup plans for coffee service at the morning session of their meeting. Though coffee is essential to some people in order for their blood to flow before 10:00 A.M., a breakdown in the delivery system wouldn't have crippled the meeting.

The rule of thumb is: If it's a prerequisite for success, you'd better make an alternate plan. If it's a frill, don't. And never do it just to put off getting started toward your objective.

Some people, including me, find it very helpful to jot down their thinking in the form of a simple flow chart. (For an extensive discussion of personal flow charts, see *Wishcraft*, by Barbara Sher, with Annie Gottlieb, Viking Press, New York, 1979.)

However you plan, do it consistently. Make sure your planning doesn't degenerate into just another list of things to accomplish. Keep your objectives uppermost in your mind. Plan to achieve them. Each plan you carry out is a small step toward your desires. Take enough small steps—and you're there.

EXERCISE 8:

Add a series of plans to your objective(s):

Mission Statement (Yes, state it again to keep it in mind):

Goal 1:   *Goal 2:*   *Goal 3:*

Objective: Objective: Objective:

Plans: Plans: Plans:

Alternates?   Alternates?   Alternates?

Objective: Objective: Objective:

Plans: Plans: Plans:

Alternates?   Alternates?   Alternates?

LAST DAY OF LOG KEEPING FOR A WHILE. HALLELUJAH!

DAYS 9–14

in which you discover new ways to solve old problems

DAY 9

The Fearsome Five: Typical Time Management Foul-ups

Congratulations! Today you take a giant step in gaining control over your time. Over the past week or so, you've defined what direction you'd like your life to take. Today, you'll begin to learn the techniques for clearing the path to your goals. With the help of those miserable, intrusive, ever-present, hassle-making time logs, you'll discover precisely why you're in the mess you're in. Subsequent chapters will show you what to do about it.

I charge my private clients megabucks and analyze their daily records for them, but since you're not paying the big fee, you'll have to schlepp through the research unescorted. It isn't hard to do, and for the compulsives among you who like to circle numbers, make check marks, and count things, this is a red-letter day indeed. Even those of you who tend toward slapdash-ery in self-examination will enjoy watching your individual time profiles emerge from the data you've collected.

There are five major areas of time mismanagement: (1) The "fritters," (2) failure to delegate, (3) filling in, (4) fatigue, and (5) frazzle.

The "fritters" can be self-induced or externally created. No matter how it originates, "frittering" is defined as taking part in activities, large or small, that divert you from your important personal objectives. Though fritters come in many shapes and sizes, they all interrupt the flow of your highest-priority work.

Typical fritters include: phone calls, incoming and outgoing; unscheduled visitors; illness or accident; mechanical failure; depletion of supplies; losing or misplacing essential items; and— my own major failing—what Dr. Dorothy Tennov, in her book *Super Self,* calls "fugue behavior."

A fugue is a type of music in which the theme is continually restated by different groups of instruments or voices. Though richly textured and complex, a fugue is essentially circular; it just keeps going round and round. Fugue behavior is similar. You begin a task, are sidetracked to another job, which suggests a new project. You return to the original task, are thrown off course again—and the behavior repeats itself over and over.

Let's suppose your task is to put away the laundry. While dumping socks in your son's drawer, you notice that he's left his camera balanced on the arm of a chair. As you interrupt your task to deposit the camera in the closet, you decide the closet is environmentally unsafe and spend the next hour mucking it out. Realizing you've been drawn away from your purpose, you return to the laundry basket, grabbing a handful of towels for the bathroom. Once there, you see the sink needs scouring. You scour it. Now the sink is so pristine the rest of the room looks dingy, so for good measure, you scrub the shower and polish the mirror—and so on. You keep starting over at the laundry, but by the time you get the stuff put away, your kids will have outgrown it. The fugue keeps playing, and another day bites the dust, done in by a fritter.

Maybe the fritters aren't much trouble for you; perhaps you victimize yourself by failing to delegate. If you find yourself doing it all because it's "simpler" or because asking for help makes you feel anxious; if you believe that if you want something done right (i.e., perfectly), you have to do it yourself; if you're afraid people won't like you if you "impose" on them, chances are you've never learned to delegate. It's a skill you must master if you don't want to end up resentful, overworked, and burned out.

It's possible that you delegate well and control interruptions but still don't accomplish your major objectives. If this is your pattern, you're probably a "filler in-er." Instead of concentrating on what really matters to you, you fill your time with low-priority occupations.

A lot of filling in may go on when you're tired and simply don't have the mental stamina to work toward objectives. At those times filling in is a sensible alternative. I schedule fill-in days at the end of long projects, before and after vacations, and at other appropriate times. Filling in is inappropriate daily behavior, however, if you want to complete important work. Ceaseless, nonproductive busyness is usually a cover-up for procrastination. Should procrastination be your weakness, you'll need to learn about your personal procrastination pattern—why and how you put things off. If you're an apt pupil, you may even learn how to postpone procrastinating.

The fourth reason for time mismanagement—fatigue—has a variety of roots. Maybe you're anemic or coming down with the flu; maybe you're depressed. Perhaps your work ethic is so deeply ingrained that you don't know how to enjoy rest and leisure; perhaps you haven't identified your daily rhythm. Whatever the causes, fatigue means that your body is trying to tell you something. You'd better listen up.

Frazzle, though related to fatigue, isn't the same thing. You may be both frazzled and fatigued, but you may be frazzled in the absence of fatigue. Frazzle refers to mental, physical, and emotional overload. It's often a characteristic of women who are blessed with extraordinary compassion and sensitivity. Do you really listen to your friends' problems? Are you the one who reconciles opposing factions at work? Are you a volunteer for the Disease-of-the-Month? Many frazzled women are impatient with social injustice and work hard to eradicate it; they make the

world a better place to live. In doing so, however, they sometimes fail to capitalize on their special talents and end up working indiscriminately and ineffectively for too many good causes.
It's not that they don't know how to say no; they simply haven't
developed a system to determine what they'll say yes to. After a
while, things get to them and they unravel. Activists, beware.
Frazzle may be lurking just around the corner. Be on the
lookout.

Now that you've been introduced, how many of the "fearsome five" do you recognize from your daily experience? Let's
jump right into identifying your hang-ups. Knowledge of the
enemy is half the battle.

EXERCISE 9:

Haul out your seven time logs, and from the information
you've collected, complete the Time Log Analysis Sheet provided on page 56. It's easiest to begin this process with Monday's record. Answer all of the questions for Monday before
moving on to Tuesday. Continue on, finishing one day at a time,
rather than shifting back and forth from column to column and
shifting back and forth from column to column and day to day.

First of all, let's see if you're frustrated by fritters. Count up
all the interruptions you charted on Monday. Assign each to an
appropriate category on the analysis sheet. Enter the totals in
the proper boxes.

To determine if failure to delegate is your stumbling block,
consider each task you performed on Monday. Ask yourself,
"Assuming this job needed to be done at all, could someone else
have done it?" Each time you answer yes, score ten points. If
the answer is no, score zero. Add them up and write the total in
Monday's column.

Do you fill in? Compare the number of low-priority tasks (3s
and 4s) you completed on Monday to the number of high-
priority accomplishments (1s and 2s). If lows outnumber highs,

score ten points. If high-priority tasks predominate, score zero. Record the number.

How tired are you? Count the number of times you listed "L" under energy level and the number of words like "shot," "beat," and "sleepy" that appear in your feeling descriptions. Total these instances and place the number in the right column.

Frazzle level is measured by totting up feeling descriptions that indicate stress, anxiety, or nervousness. See if you discover an inordinate number of words like "hassled," "annoyed," "fretful," "ticked off," and the like in the last column of your log. Nobody jogs through life constantly serene, but an overabundance of tension-filled self-descriptions can point to a problem. Enter your frazzle total at the bottom of Monday's column.

Now repeat this entire process for Tuesday through Sunday; jot down your totals for the week in each category.

When you're done, your Analysis Sheet will look something like the sample chart on page 57.

So what? What does it all mean? Generally speaking, the higher the number in the weekly total column, the more severe your mismanagement in a given area. I have listed no average scores. If you think your score is too high, it's too high.

I can tell you a lot about Sally Smith, for example, simply by glancing over her numbers. Sally has great difficulty with the telephone. She rarely delegates. Probably because of her deficiency in delegating, she fills in frequently. But Sally has strengths, too. She keeps her personal space well organized, as evidenced by her remarkably low scores regarding equipment failure, lack of materials, or misplacement of needed supplies. Sally's energetic and seems to find it easy to concentrate on one thing at a time.

Though Sally's days could stand some sprucing up, she's by no means a hopeless case. Neither are you. The next few chapters will show you how to maximize your strengths while you extricate yourself from your time tangles.

Time Log Analysis Sheet

Name: _____

	Mon.	Tues.	Wed.	Thurs.	Fri.	Sat.	Sun.	Totals
1. Fritters a. Phone interruptions								
b. People interruptions								
c. Accident/illness (self or others)								
d. Didn't have what I needed for job (lack of materials)								
e. Couldn't find what I needed for job (misplacement)								
f. Something broke down (equipment failure)								
g. Fugue behavior								
h. Other								
2. Failure to Delegate								
3. Filling in								
4. Fatigue								
5. Frazzle								

Time Log Analysis Sheet

Name: *Sally Smith*

	Mon.	Tues.	Wed.	Thurs.	Fri.	Sat.	Sun.	Totals
1. Fritters a Phone interruptions	12	6	14	9	10	6	3	60
b People interruptions	6	4	8	3	2	5	10	38
c Accident/illness (self or others)	0	0	0	0	0	0	0	0
d Didn't have what I needed for job (lack of materials)	0	0	0	0	0	0	0	0
e Couldn't find what I needed for job (misplacement)	3	1	2	0	1	1	0	8
f Something broke down (equipment failure)	0	0	0	0	0	0	0	0
g Fugue behavior	2	0	1	0	2	1	0	6
h Other								
2. Failure to Delegate	100	120	120	100	90	110	150	890
3. Filling in	10	10	10	0	0	0	10	40
4. Fatigue	4	3	5	1	2	0	2	17
5. Frazzle	2	1	3	1	0	1	3	11

DAY 10

The Fritters and the Fritterers

Do you suffer from the fritters? Is your day a series of interruptions punctuated by occasional productivity? Does your mother call three times a day? Do co-workers crowd around your desk? Do your kids clamor incessantly? Does your copier or vacuum cleaner spend more time in the shop than on the job?

Well, my friend, for fast, fast, fast relief, follow the simple instructions in this chapter. They don't fizz and they aren't recommended by nine out of ten doctors, but they're effective against the symptoms of the fritters.

Though there are many individual fritters, they may all be divided into two distinct groups: thing-caused fritters and people-caused fritters.

Impossible as it sometimes seems, we can exert some measure of control over those inanimate objects that appear to rule our lives and are so often the targets of our anger.

Take, for example, the telephone. ("I'm going to rip the damn thing right out of the wall!") Though you can't regulate the whims of those who ring you up (almost always at inconvenient times), you can decide whether or not you'll knuckle under to a bell.

Deputize others to handle the phone. Kids can be wonderful at-home secretaries, diverting callers and taking messages. They'll need some instruction in polite telephone procedures, of course, but once trained, they're invaluable helpers.

You're the only one home? I strongly urge the purchase of an inexpensive answering machine with a call-monitoring switch. You can attach it to your phone, turn up the monitoring equipment, and hear who's calling without breaking your routine. Should your prefer to catch your messages later, just turn off the monitor and work in peace.

I advocate a machine to deal with this particular thing-problem because many women find it difficult to disregard a ringing telephone, particularly if family is far-flung. There are some hardy souls, however, who can ignore the insistent jangle. I congratulate them and advise continuation of this habit.

When even the ring disturbs your concentration, unplug the phone. Don't take it off the hook. I don't know what leaving it off the hook does to the "great grid," but whatever it is, it causes Ma Bell anxiety attacks.

A more assertive telephone management strategy is to schedule telephone hours and to let people know when you'll be available to talk to them. Log your calls for a few days to find out who your major interrupters are. On their next call, explain to them that you're trying a new time management method and that after a certain date, you'll be taking calls only at specified hours. You might even make appointments with special people within those times. One of my clients made such a schedule with her mother. Mother knew that that time was hers, she enjoyed the daily brief chats, and she stopped calling my client several times a day.

My pediatrician had daily telephone hours from 7:00 to 8:30 A.M. It was a great relief to be able to reach him first thing in the morning, and I know it made his office run more smoothly. (He also scheduled ten minutes at the end of each hour for call-backs to patients who'd needed his advice within that hour. It was terrific. No sitting for hours by the phone trying to find out what to do for Johnny's cough or waiting all day for a prescription refill. This man understood the value of time—his own and his patients'.)

At work, your phone problems are different, but solutions are similar. Your secretary can certainly screen or hold calls. You can schedule telephone availability hours and call-back times.

If you're the secretary, it's a fact of life that your work is going to be interrupted. The position description should reflect that your job is to do twenty-seven different things while being constantly interrupted. There are ways to minimize the problem, though. The company operator can hold calls. Should there be no operator, but many secretaries, you can institute floor-duty hours, during which one secretary is responsible for screening calls for everyone. Sometimes in a boss-secretary dyad, the boss answers her own phone for a while, so that you can crank out the paperwork or whatever. This arrangement has the added benefit of giving the boss a glimpse of what your day is *really* like, and it sometimes impresses the heck out of clients.

These techniques demonstrate graphically that you don't have to be a martyr, burning with impatience while somebody prattles on at the other end of the wire. You can set limits to tyranny by telephone.

Other thing-caused fritters that can reduce you to confusion and cursing include getting all revved up to do a job and finding you have none of the needed supplies, or completing half the assignment and running out of necessary materials. This is the easiest thing-problem to fix. A simple, continuous inventory will show you at a glance whether to go ahead with a project or to wait until you've gathered the proper tools.

It may be that you have all the supplies you need to perform a task, but you can't find them. Creating a "home" for each frequently mislaid article can end this state of affairs. If you can't learn to put things away in their "homes" (I toss my car keys everywhere and can never find my glasses), spend some money on duplicates. You'll make up the expenditure in time no longer wasted tracking your belongings through the Land of the Lost. Extras are useful too if your supplies are frequently escorted from their niches by improvident family or co-workers.

You can also save time by spending money in the case of equipment failure. Machines, equipment, and labor-saving devices may sometimes seem part of a giant conspiracy designed to trip you up; they sense intuitively the most devastating time to blow a gasket. Unless you're trained in repair work, your frustration factor rises proportionately to the number of days (or weeks) the repair requires.

Some breakdowns just happen, but with only a little thinking ahead, a sizable number could be averted. Preventive maintenance of cars, washing machines, typewriters—whatever is essential to your daily work—should be a given. Because of the emphasis in this country on disposability (the virtue of which is arguable), you, like many others, may have forgotten the concept of caring for possessions. Do you mistreat things until they go on the fritz and then grumble about down-time? The old adage about a stitch in time became an old adage because it's true. A service contract might save your sanity, and a regularly scheduled auto tune-up could save your life. Investing an hour in maintenance now will pay dividends later.

Inventories, maintenance, and duplicates are obvious solutions to uncomplicated problems. People-caused dilemmas are another can of worms entirely. People drop by unannounced; children have monumental needs; co-workers want to load you up with their overflow work; friends lay claim to your leisure hours. You value and love all these people, but you still want to pursue your own goals. How can you do so without stomping all over others' feelings? What do you do, for example, about people who show up at your doorstep without warning?

According to Emily Post, it's okay for the butler to tell visitors you're not at home, even if you're sitting right there in the living room polishing Mummy's tiara. Unfortunately, my butler ran off with the chambermaid, so now I have to open my own door. But I don't always do it. Oddly, though I feel compelled to answer a telephone, a knock on the door doesn't produce the same effect. Since news of accident, injury, or disaster rarely comes on foot, I have no anxiety about remaining behind my locked front door. A peephole helps me decide my course of action. If it shows me a face I want to see, the door is flung wide. Otherwise, I go about my business.

Some people-interruptions don't come from outsiders. Kids are notorious intruders. It's up to you to keep this behavior within bounds. In doing so, there are several points to consider.

First, I assume you didn't have children in order to neglect them. Children require your attention, and I think that the "quality time" we hear advocated so often is a cop-out. Sometimes kids need a large quantity of time as well, and they don't always ask for it when it's convenient. Some interruptions are unavoidable.

But not all. Kids can be taught at an early age that Mom needs some quiet time to accomplish important work. A regularly scheduled individual playtime is good for children. Armed with suitable materials, your child can benefit from solitude; it teaches self-reliance and creativity. You don't have to be there every minute monitoring, checking, passing judgment. Leave the kid alone to dream, to consider possibilities, to think. It frees up his or her imagination and your time.

Children should also be required to respect a closed door. When I was just starting my company, I worked at home in the den. The room had no door, so the children wandered in and out at will, bombarding me with such startling bulletins as the fact that they'd found a bird's nest, Ceci wasn't home and neither was Richard, and wow, the dog was really shedding. Since installing a door wasn't possible, I hung a sign that said, "This is a door. It is closed. Do not enter except in an emergency. An emergency is somebody bleeding or barfing." The sign worked beautifully, and I had two hours of uninterrupted planning and research time every morning. Once they realized that I really needed the time for business purposes, the children began to guard my quiet hours jealously. They were so helpful that four years later I still have my office at home, it still has no door, and I no longer have to post the sign. Kids will almost always measure up if they know what you want and why.

Such is not the the case with adults. They barge right into your office, gossiping or weeping and wailing over their personal problems and almost always neglect to ask whether this is a good time for you. Of course, you can't send them to their rooms to cool down, but there are some useful coping methods available to you.

Presumably adults are grown up enough to handle candor. If you haven't a free moment to give them, say so. Tactfully. Diplomatically. And very clearly. Schedule a later appointment if the situation warrants such action. Often simply suggesting an appointment to further discuss the topic at hand will cause the interrupter to reassess the importance of the present conversation.

While it is essential to be available to people, that availability needn't be constant. Schedule blocks of time when you will be on call to your staff or co-workers. Open your door during these intervals.

Then close it and left officemates know that in addition to accessibility hours, you also need uninterrupted thinking time. During your quiet time, only the business equivalent of bleeding or barfing should be permitted to intrude.

If you're the secretary rather than the boss, you might suggest some of these options to your employer. Together you can form a dynamic, productive team.

There is one significant interrupter we haven't mentioned, and she's generally the one who impedes your work the most. Take a look in the mirror. The face you see very well may be the head honcho of the interruption hierarchy. All the ways you're interrupted by outsiders are also ways you may interrupt yourself. Perhaps you come between yourself and your work by telephoning. Monitor your outgoing calls for a few days and note any calling patterns that develop. Why do you make calls? For information? To make or confirm appointments? Your secretary can handle information gathering and can certainly set up appointments for you. Children can make their own doctor, dentist, and hair-cut appointments, after consultation with you or their dad. They can also cancel these appointments, by themselves, should the need arise.

Do you substitute a phone conversation for an unpleasant task? I used to place calls like mad right after dinner because I couldn't face the thought of scraping, stacking, washing, and scouring. Other women report similar behavior in the face of a deadline, a meeting with the boss, or the beginning of a major project. When you become aware that you're using the telephone as an avoidance mechanism, stop at once. Remember that the callee herself may be wishing she could find a cure for *phonus interruptus.*

For women who work at home, excessive outgoing calls can be a manifestation of "housewives' phone-itis." In this country, homemakers are often almost criminally isolated. Some view the aloneness as a creative challenge and deal with it productively; others are lonely, and for them the telephone becomes a virtual lifeline. They spend literally hours on the phone, forcing friends and relatives to serve as unpaid counselors, exhausting both themselves and their listeners. The remedy for this condition is reinvolvement in life outside the house, no matter how difficult it may be to arrange. No one thrives in solitary confinement; why do you think they use it to such advantage in prisons?

The same dynamics that govern telephone interruptions may impel you to become the too-frequent visitor, the interrupter of others. This behavior should trigger a vigorous self-appraisal. Are you bored? Unchallenged? Procrastinating? Throwing a monkey wrench into everyone else's day won't resolve your dilemma. You will eventually have to confront the underlying issues, and there's no time like the present.

The present is also the time to take action against the most complicated self-induced fritter—fugue behavior. The only sure cure for this malady is total concentration—complete attention to the job at hand. I once had a sorority sister who was a 4.0 student, a cheerleader, and an officer in student government. She studied rarely, but when she did, she was fully focused on her research. She was not distractable. This same resistance to distraction can make all the difference to a fugue player. In his book, *How to Meditate*, Lawrence LeShan describes the Little Way of St. Theresa, which

> consisted of doing all the small tasks of every day life with the knowledge that each one is a part of the total harmony of the universe. They were done with love and *total concentration* and the attitude that this task was the most important thing to be doing at that moment.

Metaphysics aside, complete concentration yields the benefits of greatly increased efficiency and a sense of pleasure in the present moment. I often recommend simple meditation as a starting place for overcoming fugue behavior. Meditation is a discipline not quickly learned, but the gains in organizational skill are worth the effort.

Another way of tackling the problem is to set a timer and to work at only one task until the bell goes off. Reset and continue on to the next task. While not so pleasurable as internal quiet concentration, the timer technique achieves the same results— the completion of tasks in sequence. This routine can serve as a stopgap measure until you learn to emulate St. Theresa.

By now, I'm sure you've detected my bias that self-knowledge, preplanning, and a calm assertiveness can minimize the effects of the most persistent fritters. I wouldn't want to give you the impression, however, that every set of circumstances can be controlled. People have accidents. They get sick. They die. When these sorrows visit your house, it is useless to consider what you could or should have done. "If only" is the biggest time-waster or all. It takes time to recover, time to heal, time to grieve. Enter into the process, cope as well as you can, accept what help is offered, and treat yourself with compassion.

Enforced idleness can give you a unique opportunity for introspection, rest, and refreshment of spirit. These kinds of activities may even hasten your recovery. Beating yourself about unfinished work and unmet deadlines will only heighten anxiety and delay recuperation. Let go for a time. When you've returned to full strength, you'll work with a new perspective and competence.

EXERCISE 10:

From your Time Analysis Sheet, identify your biggest fritter. Today, take two actions to combat it. Continue these actions until Day 21.

DAY 11

Delegation: Dumpers, Saints, and Managers

In their book, *About Time*, management experts Alec Mackenzie and Kay Cronkite Waldo state that delegation is "one of the most critical of all time saving activities." They list as its benefits: (1) the extension of effectiveness, (2) the release of time for more important work, (3) the maintenance of decision making at the lowest possible level, and (4) the development of subordinates' initiative, skills, competence, etc.

If delegation is such a hot deal, why do women keep admitting that they do it rarely, if at all? Why would women ignore or actively resist a technique that is so potentially liberating? Several theories have been advanced. One speculates that women don't delegate because they're afraid of failure. In other words, women are too timid to delegate. Delegation is a risk. There is a possibility of rebellion among those delegated to. In the face of such a reaction, it's postulated that women lack the assertiveness to make delegation stick. Rather than endure confrontation and a subsequent backing down, many women avoid delegation altogether.

Diametrically opposed to this hypothesis is the notion that women don't delegate because they're afraid of success. They worry that the "delegatees" will do so well they'll put the "delegator" out of a job. The team will become so strong they'll usurp the leader's role. Why would a reasonable woman put herself in that position? It's hard enough to keep a job. Delegate it away? No thanks!

Allied to this fear of success is the fear of relinquishing power. Women have traditionally held less power than men. Performing a task—having mastery and ownership of it—is a form of power. For some women, delegating functions over which they have control is tantamount to parting with the only power they have. The woman in the sickbed who berates her husband's grocery-shopping style has a power problem as well as a virus.

Some women, it's said, have a streak of perfectionism a mile wide. They can't stand to see a job done haphazardly, no matter what the result. To spare themselves the headache of witnessing subordinates' errors during the learning process, they don't delegate. It's less painful to keep on doing it all themselves.

All these theories have a kernel of truth in them. There are timid women, insecure women, power-starved women, perfectionist women. I think, however, that there's a more compelling reason women fail to delegate, and it has little to do with their psychological states. I believe women don't delegate because 1 they don't know what delegation really is, and 2 they don't know how to do it.

According to the dictionary, to delegate is "to commit or entrust (powers, authority, etc.) to another as an agent or representative." A delegate is "a person sent with authority to represent another." The key to these definitions is, of course, authority. Women unaware that authority is the capstone of delegation fall into two categories: Dumpers and Saints.

A dumper is a woman who rids herself of all the onerous tasks in her job description by assigning them at random to whoever happens by. Since she never gives away authority commensurate with the tasks, her delegates are nothing more than beasts of burden, with no stake or interest in the outcome of a job. Giving someone a chore that you don't want and he or she doesn't either isn't delegating. It's dumping.

Standing at the opposite pole from the Dumper is the Saint. Reared to believe that nice girls don't impose on others, she views all delegation as "bothering" someone else. Rather than be rude and "ask a favor" from a busy person, she attends to every detail herself; she gives away no functions whatsoever. She's easy to work for if you don't mind a no-growth situation and can stand occasional emotional flare-ups from a boss who doesn't understand why she "can't get any help around here." While the Dumper may find herself with a full-scale slave revolt on her hands, the Saint is more likely to check into a quiet room at the local laughing academy, completely unstrung but congratulating herself for her "good girlhood."

There are women, though, who comprehend the authority angle of delegation. They have the whole concept clearly in mind, but they can't translate it into action. For them, and for you, here's the WOMANHOURS Way to Dandy Delegation.

First, determine whether the job you're delegating needs to be done at all. If delegation has failed for you before, it may be because you've asked others to carry out duties that you didn't need to do, but neither did anyone else. Don't delegate makework. (Don't do it either.) Before proceeding with delegation, ask yourself, "Does this job need to be done by anyone?"

If the answer is yes, the next question is "Why me?" This is a serious issue. Do you have specific skills, talents, and competences that make you absolutely the best person to discharge this responsibility? Are there real advantages to be gained by your being in command? If not, look around for the person most qualified by ability and aptitude to do the job.

The third question is, "Have I learned the ins and outs of this job so thoroughly that I could teach them to another, and will learning this task be a growth experience for him or her?" Much of delegation is teaching someone how to do something, and ideally you delegate to the person most qualified to learn who will find some challenge in the learning.

Now that you know what you want and for whom you're looking, the issue becomes how to drag him or her aboard.

As is so often the case, the essence of cooperation is communication. Have a forthright talk with the designated delegate. Share what you hope to accomplish by this division of responsibility. Make desired results the focus of the initial interview. Ask for the delegate's suggestions. Try to get him or her to assume some ownership of the situation.

Your delegate will need information in order to do the job, so arrange a teaching schedule to impart your knowledge of policies and procedures. Set a deadline for the systems to be learned and the delegate's new responsibilities to begin. At the same time, work out a reporting method for him or her to inform you of progress and problems. These reports will also allow you to oversee the delegate without controlling the problem itself.

Let others know that your delegate is now in charge of this chunk of your previously held duties. Delegation doesn't work if others are constantly end-running the designate. Publicly give your delegate authority and credibility. Now, get out of the way. Let the delegate work, without your hovering and hot breath on his or her neck. Don't start fretting because your replacement does things differently from you. Of course he or she does; he or she is not you. How the job is done isn't your business anymore. As long as the desired results are being achieved, style differences should be overlooked. Of course, if the delegate's style is alienating customers or causing other personnel problems, you'll need a corrective interview to deal with these issues. Otherwise, leave things alone.

At this point, sit back and enjoy, and don't forget to acknowledge publicly a job well done. Give yourself a pat on the back, too. By training and developing a subordinate, you've just become a real manager.

EXERCISE 11:

Have you been a Saint or a Dumper? Become a manager today. Delegate a task you've never considered giving up before. Stay with this delegation until Day 21. Monitor your reaction.

DAY 12

Pareto's Principle and the Perils of Pauline's Procrastination

So what do you do if you know what you want to do but you don't do it? Somehow instead of pursuing your goals, you stuff your days full of busy work, putting off the gratification that comes with achieving your heart's desire. You thrash around, drowning in a sea of low-priority chores. You need a life preserver to keep your head above water at least long enough to discover why you behave the way you do. If you can figure that out, perhaps you can backstroke your way to shore.

I'm going to throw out two lifelines, one labeled *list making* and the other *procrastination*. Grab either one or both and I'll try to reel you in.

Though you may yet feel a little over your head concerning all you have to do and the amount of time you have to do it, you're better off than those women still stuck with task-role definitions. You've begun to move away from this method of operation; you've set goals, forecast objectives, and dealt with some serious time management issues. It's right at this point that many of my clients think they've come to the end of the line. Somehow the old tasks keep cluttering up the landscape. After all, you can't delegate everything. There are still nitty-gritty chores that require action. In even the most well-organized life, those maintenance chores can eat up a big chunk of time. How do you cut them down to size?

There's a classy little rule in sales and management circles that I found most useful when I was struggling with this problem. It's called the "Pareto Principle," and in Alan Lakein's book, *How to Get Control of Your Time and Your Life*, he puts it like this: "If all items are arranged in order of value, 80 percent of the value would come from only 20 percent of the items, while the remaining 20 percent of the value would come from 80 percent of the items."

In its pure form, the Pareto Principle is confusing, but it becomes crystal clear when translated into everyday terms and aplied to a wide range of daily activities. For example, when you were logging your telephone interruptions, you probably found that roughly 80 percent of them were caused by approximately 20 percent of all the people who called. If you're the family cook, it's likely that 80 percent of the recipes you prepare come from 20 percent of the cookbooks you own. Unless you've carefully coordinated your clothes, you probably wear 20 percent of your total wardrobe 80 percent of the time. And I would bet that if you're a daily list maker, the "must-do," high-priority items on your list comprise about 20 percent of the total number of tasks listed.

Though daily list making is helpful as a memory jog, I think it can be a real guilt producer if every single chore is catalogued. With each daily duty carefully penciled in, the tendency is to feel that success equals a line drawn through each entry. In fact, that's the least effective way to use such a list. A "to-do" list that works well is short. You will find an example of an effective list at the end of this chapter.

All daily lists should start with a brief statement of your objectives. Making such a statement each day helps to keep objectives clear and focused. With your objective statement written, jot down an inventory of tasks you'd like to complete. Next note appointments you've scheduled for that day. Now identify the 20 percent of tasks and appointments that will advance your objectives. Finally, mesh together your high-value tasks and your scheduled appointments in a combined list and schedule. Leave some blocks of time to handle things that "just come up." Wedge in a few mundane chores (get bread, buy shower gift) and you're done. That's your total list. Completion of just the major items guarantees you an 80 percent return on your day. All the rest is gravy. A consistent 80 percent effectiveness rate is good enough to make you an exhibit at managerial seminars from coast to coast. This kind of achievement assures goal attainment.

This new-style list making may sound complicated at first, but after a few days' practice you'll have a to-do list that's short, to the point, and a real springboard to productive time use. You can't miss!

I take that back. There's a way you can miss, and I've watched women do it. They delineate very carefully the tasks that will propel them toward their goals, and then they don't perform them. They hem and haw; they stall; they put it off.

There are almost as many types and styles of procrastination as there are types and styles of people, but there are two major classifications of procrastination—conscious and unconscious.

Perhaps you know that you do your best work under pressure. When a major project is coming up, you put off beginning your tasks until the last minute. Then, in a blaze of glory, you perform brilliantly and complete your required assignment by the deadline. That's conscious procrastination. You've analyzed yourself and your patterns of functioning and have made a rational decision to accommodate your style. So long as it doesn't screw up an entire department's output, give you an ulcer, or result in a passel of missed deadlines, it's right for you.

A more devious kind of conscious procrastination involves putting off a job until someone else, frustrated by your inactivity, leaps into the breach and carries out your task. Kids use this kind of manipulation very successfully. They know that if they can just hold out long enough, eventually Mom will crack and clean up the room or lug the trash out herself. Don't get sucked into the game. A reasonable deadline should be set and corrective action instituted in the event the deadline isn't met. Don't use this kind of procrastination against others either. Far better to turn down an obligation at the outset than to maneuver others into relieving you of your freely chosen responsibilities. An assertive refusal is respected; weaseling out is not.

Unconscious procrastination means that you know you're putting things off, but you don't know why. To determine what psychological stance you're operating from, it's helpful to discover what psychological payoff you're getting from the practice of postponement.

In *How to Put More Time in Your Life,* Dr. Dru Scott suggests that excitement and stimulation are potent motivators in procrastination behavior. If you're bored by your job; if you feel like an insignificant cog in the wheel of commerce; if you're wiped out by the drudgery of housekeeping, you may crave excitement. Throwing sand in the gears of your employment or subjecting your home to inspection by the Board of Health are drastic methods to find the excitement you require. It's much more useful to examine your need for stimulation and then meet that need creatively and positively.

Procrastination is a powerful attention getter. A woman whose contributions or talents are taken for granted—a woman who feels faceless—can become well known very quickly just by not quite getting around to her assigned responsibilities. It's like the child's tantrum that produces a spanking—even negative attention is preferable to no attention. But positive attention is best of all. Spend the prodigious energy it takes to procrastinate in seeking inventive solutions to your problems.

It's possible you're postponing a task because you're afraid you'll fail. The job might be something you've never tried before. It may involve dealing with people whose name or position intimidates you. The magnitude of the job may overwhelm you. I think the answer to this type of difficulty is the widely known "baby-step" approach. Break the job down into easily achievable discrete segments and act on one segment at a time.

For example, suppose your task is to sell a particular program to a community bigwig—one with a corner office, two windows, Queen Anne furniture, and an oriental rug. You're so terrorized by the thought of interviewing Mr. or Ms. Big that you're immobilized. You stall and delay until you lose your opportunity, and then you kick yourself.

The baby-step technique reduces this alarming proposition to manageable size. You might first research the person you're trying to interest. What has he or she done in the past that might predispose him or her to your project? You can ferret out the facts from the library or from friends. That's not so scary. Next you could write a letter outlining your project and asking for an appointment. That's no big deal either. A few days later, you call the secretary and make the appointment. You've placed phone calls before, haven't you? No sweat. Next comes the actual interview. Though you might have butterflies, the meeting will go smoothly because you're prepared, and the prospect knows why you've come. He or she is at least interested enough to let you in the door. Walk into that impressive office, state your case concisely, obtain the support of the bigwig, thank him or her for the time and attention and leave. It's done, and it could be the beginning of a beautiful friendship. If you think small enough, almost anything is possible.

It's conceivable that you defer action on a project not because you're afraid of failure, but because you're fearful that you'll do well. Success, like going over Niagara Falls in a barrel, is very exciting, but risky. Maybe you'd rather paddle a canoe in the headwaters, where you know the locations of the rocks. Not every woman is possessed by a driving will to "make it." Perhaps you're satisfied with more modest attainments. I would be cautious about caution, though. Deeply felt satisfaction with your lot in life is one thing; a fear-ridden stagnation is another. A leap into the unknown is never easy, and sometimes it's painful, but no guts, no glory. When you've arrived at the bottom of the Falls with your barrel battered, but your skin intact, the trip's been worth it.

Some women—a small minority—procrastinate in order to deny themselves satisfaction. Their self-image is in such disarray that they see themselves as unworthy of the satisfaction a completed project would bring them. Obviously, in this case, procrastination is just the tip of the iceberg. It's an indication of an internal conflict that's certainly beyond the scope of my expertise. The effective use of time is impossible in such a climate of self-rejection. Only after this skein of misperceptions is untangled does time management begin to make sense. A constant undercurrent of "unworthiness" that impairs your ability to function should start you off in the direction of a qualified helping professional—an M.D., a psychologist, a member of the clergy. There are some good books around, but there's also a lot of trash, so I'd be leery about self-diagnosis and pop-psych cures. If you find a helpful book, use it in conjunction with counseling, not as a replacement. You may need only short-term assistance, but short term or long haul, don't be afraid to ask for help. The results are worth the effort.

EXERCISE 12:

1 If you're a list maker, try your hand at a new-style list from today until Day 21. If you're not a list maker, you have no bad habits to break. Just begin keeping a to-do list today. (See sample on page 78–79.)

or

2 Take the first baby step toward achieving a long-delayed

goal or job. Continue one baby step a day until the task is completed.

A To-Do List That Works

Day's objectives: 1. To finish fund-raising responsibility
                   2. To continue exercise program

List 1: Tasks you'd like to complete today

 1. Call Janet re bazaar
 2. Get bread
 3. Pick up dry cleaning
*4. Write copy for fund-raising
    brochure
*5. Get fund-raising target
    figure from Judy

 6. Clean living room
 7. Iron shirts
 8. Buy baby present for shower
 9. Visit Mother
10. Buy résumé guide

List 2: Appointments

 1. Mary to doctor—8:00 A.M.
 2. Carpool—4:00 P.M.
*3. Aerobics class—7:00 P.M.

Now identify the 20 percent that matter most:

*1. Write copy for fund-raising brochure
*2. Get fund-raising target figure from Judy
*3. Attend aerobics class at 7:00 P.M.

Combined List and Schedule

7:00 A.M.
8:00—Mary to doctor and back to school
9:00
10:00 ⎫
11:00 ⎬ —Write copy for brochure; get target figure from Judy
12:00 M. ⎬
1:00 P.M ⎭
2:00
3:00
4:00—Carpool to band practice
5:00
6:00
7:00 ⎫
8:00 ⎬ —Aerobics class
9:00
10:00

All the times that are vacant on this schedule are available for lower-value tasks, but even if everything doesn't get done, the day's 80 percent objectives have been met by the completion of two tasks and one appointment. Completing your high-value objectives gives you a real psychological boost.

DAY 13

Fatigue: The Woman's Companion

"I'm so tired all the time! I keep asking myself if my activities are worth this. I'd give anything to sleep for about two days. What can I do about this?"

That's one of my clients talking, and there's a whole range of things she can "do about this," but she can select appropriate measures only if she unearths the reasons for her weariness. More sleep won't help her if she's out of sync with her daily rhythm; vitamins will profit her nothing if she's just in a rut. So, once again, analysis precedes action.

Fatigue springs from a variety of circumstances. Some reasons for fatigue are simple; some are complex. Let's start with the easy stuff.

Overwork can cause fatigue. (You already know that? Well, I told you this part would be easy.) Slaving away eighteen to twenty hours a day is bound to produce fatigue unless you're Thomas Alva Edison. There are some fortunate folks who thrive on six or fewer hours of sleep a night, but they're rare, and they're usually geniuses. Though everyone's sleep pattern is unique, some studies indicate that seven to eight hours rest is optimum for most people. Less than that can create a sleep deficit, and a woman operating with a deficit is likely to work inefficiently. She's prone to lapses of concentration and may even be susceptible to accidents and injury.

Extralong hours that are a temporary condition with a defined endpoint probably won't result in lasting harm, but I would question any woman who complains that her clock habitually runs eighteen hours a day. What are you doing with those hours? Moonlighting? Studying for an advanced degree? Serving the community? Worrying? Is what you're working for worth the wear and tear on your body? Is the time limit for the achievement of your goal realistic? Should it be lengthened? Are you locked into prescribed duties or could you arrange some innovative alternatives? Could you trade, barter, buy, or co-op some time for rest?

Rest and relaxation are indispensable aspects of a balanced life, but some women treat them like the plague. I've had clients actually apologize when their time logs indicated a rest period. I've read statements like, "Sorry, this probably isn't the best time of the day for me to rest, but I just had to," or "This isn't the most effective use of my time, but I'm exhausted." These kinds of declarations let me know that my client is either a Puritan or a Wonder Woman. Puritans still hang onto the idea that relaxation is somehow a sin and that idle hands are lazy hands. In fact, there's a world of difference between those two words. Even if there weren't, occasional laziness is a faculty of being human, and it's a real waste of time to apologize for your humanity.

Wonder Women, as mentioned in Section 1, don't ease off because they're intent on proving their strength. Rest indicates weakness, giving in, frailty. To those Wonder Women among you, I can only reiterate: *STOP IT!* Wonder Woman is a clear and present danger to both your physical and emotional health. She's more powerful than you are and will wear you down eventually. Surrender now. Live within your bodily means.

Your body wasn't designed to run flat out at all times. No machine (and that's what the body is—an intricate machine) can sustain constant high-speed performance. If you want results from a piece of equipment, you have to treat the mechanism with care. You can't ask it to deliver beyond capacity without wrecking it. You know that metal fatigue can cause steel to shatter into shards and fly in all directions. Person fatigue can do the same to you.

If rest is so necessary, why is it that inactivity is so enervating? If you rarely run your engine at high speed, you may well wonder how you can possibly be tired. Have you ever said, "Gosh, I don't know why I'm so pooped. I haven't done a thing all day." That's why you're so pooped. Just as your body sometimes requires repose, it also craves exercise and physical as well as mental gymnastics. Neglecting energetic bodily movement results in a dull mind and a listless spirit. If you've been resting, but it isn't helping your fatigue, try activity. A brisk walk, a bike ride, dancing, even a few sit-ups can go a long way toward eliminating exhaustion.

Some forward-thinking companies have installed exercise complexes for their employees, particularly those who spend the majority of their time on the job sitting or standing. I've seen no studies on whether or not such programs have increased employee productivity, but it wouldn't surprise me if they had. You will certainly want to take advantage of such a facility at your place of employment.

From my personal experience, I can testify to the benefits of vigorous exercise. With the possible exception of being in active labor, writing this book has been the most tiring experience of my life, and exercise breaks have been essential to keeping the thought process from grinding to an embarrassing halt.

Some women wear themselves out unnecessarily by missing their rhythm. Each person has fairly well-defined high- and low-energy periods each day. My own pattern, for example, is: 6:00 A.M. to 10:00 A.M.—very high; 10:00 A.M. TO 12:00 M.—moderately high; 12:00 M. to 2:00 P.M.—moderately low; 2:00 P.M.

to 4:00 P.M.—barely conscious; 4:00 P.M. to 7:00 P.M.—building momentum; 7:00 P.M. to 9:00 P.M.—moderately high; 9:00 P.M. to 11:00 P.M.—a sudden drop-off to low and sleepy. Given this knowledge, it would be silly of me to spend the morning hours in routine tasks or, conversely, to try to master difficult, creative, or unfamiliar work in the mid- to late afternoon. I barely know my name at those hours! Whatever tasks I choose to do should mesh with my level of functioning.

Frequently, though, "morning women" will use those peak periods to wash dishes, sweep floors, or do laundry—to get it all out of the way before starting the day's major occupations. Unfortunately, by the time they get around to those occupations, their performance may be slipshod or impaired because they've missed the crest of their energy wave. A couple of mundane chores may prime the pump for effective action—a writer I know always cleans off her desk before starting to work—but filling up an entire high-energy period with such minutiae wastes creative abilities and tires you out needlessly. Should you be an afternoon functioner, you could, of course, consign your mindless tasks to your mindless morning hours.

The point is that matching your energy level to the complexity or importance of a job is a quick and easy way to reduce exhaustion. Working against yourself all day long, just because this "is the way I've always done it" will result in a loss of productivity and an increase in fatigue. Catch your rhythm. Make it work for you. Exploit your "prime time."

Until now, we've been considering biological causes of fatigue. There can often be a psychological cause as well. Its name is depression. Depression has many identifying features, but one of the most common is overwhelming weariness of both body and mind. Sometimes this malaise is severe enough to send you to the doctor. You go through the standard tests and everything comes back within normal limits, but you're still completely wrung out. Now what? If there's been no recent alteration of your life condition (a new baby, a job change, moving, etc.) that could account for your lassitude, I'd nose around for other symptoms. Do you feel tired because your sleep pattern has been interrupted by insomnia or early-morning waking? Is your listlessness accompanied by irritability, loss of interest in other people, and lesser satisfaction with pursuits you once enjoyed? Do you cry excessively? Have you recently lost (or gained) a good deal of weight? Has there been a change in your interest in sex? Are you burdened with a constant sense of disappointment? Is it difficult for you to concentrate—or even to think? When you do think, are your thoughts sometimes bizarre or frightening? Have you contemplated suicide? All of these conditions point to depression.

Women in the throes of depression often feel weird, disconnected, and alone. They are certain that nobody else in recorded history has ever felt so dreadful and lived to tell about it. As a matter of fact, countless women have, and have returned to full capacity, stronger and better than they were before their depressive episode. You're not alone; at any given moment many of your sisters are suffering too. You may not know it because women can be superb actresses. They have to be; a "hysterical woman" tag can mess up employment opportunities and spoil relationships with friends and family. I've had three major episodes of depression, and no one outside my family knew it until I decided to go public after the fact.

There are many definitions of depression, the classic being "anger turned inward." I don't think anger is the total story, but I do believe that most depressions have an angry aspect. Some believe that depression is chemically based; certainly the body chemistry is altered when these episodes occur. Depression could be what Maggie Scarf calls in *Unfinished Business* "a failure in adaptation" to a particular set of life circumstances, or a result of "thinking [about yourself] in an illogical, negative manner," as David Burns suggests in *Feeling Good*. It's a complicated issue. Unless your depression is mild and self-limiting—a sort of extended case of "the blues," the complexity of possible causes may require professional help.

From my emphasis on professional intervention in this and

the previous chapter, you may wonder if I always cop out to the mental health establishment. I don't, and in fact believe that it's desirable to try to examine and solve your own problems. When those problems overwhelm you, however, it seems to me to be the best use of time to avail yourself of the skill and training of a professional. If you were lost in the wilds of the African jungle, you'd do better with a guide than with your own machete and only a vague idea of where you were going. If the hardships of daily living are making a jungle of your life, hire a pathfinder.

Fatigue, whatever its source, can never be completely eliminated, but self-awareness and adaptation can help provide an energy transfusion.

EXERCISE 13:

Using your time logs, find your high-energy levels. Then investigate what activities you were performing at these peak periods. How are you using your prime time? Today, and through Day 21, rearrange a comfortable number of tasks to accommodate your prime time. Break a habit today!

DAY 14
The Old Frazzle-Dazzle

And now comes "frazzle"—that feeling of "ungluedness," the anxiety of stretching yourself in too many directions at once, the sense of being caught in the vortex of other people's needs and expectations. You're cranky, annoyed, jumpy. There are too many phone calls, too many deadlines, and too many demands. All you want to do is punch out before you punch *somebody* out.

Frazzle is almost always the result of overcommitment. To be overcommitted, you don't have to serve on twelve boards, two commissions, and a council. If your life circumstances are particularly stressful at a given time, even one outside responsibility may be the last straw.

Yet responsibilities seem to seek you out. There is so much that needs to be done—in the schools and churces, in government and law, in health and human services. You want to help. How do you offer the time you have to give without getting in over your head? How do you give your time freely, yet still remain free? What is the difference between full commitment and overcommitment?

Overcommitment usually begins like this: your best friend, Sue, is head of fund raising for the new learning center at the high school. She's looking for committee members, and what she needs desperately is a treasurer. You have kids in the school, you think the learning center is an exciting concept, and you want to be a good friend and citizen. So, even though detail work and math have never been your long suits, you feel an obligation to accept the job. Six months later, you're agonizing over the books, hassling the bank about a lost deposit ticket, and hating yourself for taking on this idiotic proposition. You weren't right for it; it wasn't right for you. You did the wrong job for the wrong reasons.

Unless you become aware of what's happening, you may continue to allow wrong reasons to dominate your choice of activities. Perhaps you consent to join organizations because they're prestigious, or work on "socially acceptable" projects you don't really care about. Maybe you trail your friends into too many programs, until one day you've had it. You realize that all your time is being eaten up by other people's priorities. Your own agenda is blank because you're always working on someone else's. Things you might enjoy doing remain undone; classes that interest you aren't taken; spontaneous family fun has disappeared. Welcome to Frazzleland.

Many time managers will tell you that your salvation from overcommitment lies in the word "no." I've had clients who taped a little "no" sign above their telephones or wrote out a gracious turndown and read it whenever people called to ask for their assistance. That kind of arrangement will certainly prevent overcommitment, but it's just as choiceless as saying "yes" to everything that comes along. Constant nay saying boxes you in and closes down many opportunities for growth. Also, if you've been reared in a cultural or religious ethos that values helping others, consistent refusal to do so can stir up plenty of anxiety and guilt.

What's needed then is not instruction in how to say "no," but a system that allows you to say "yes" to full commitment in a few areas. Full commitment means that you've assessed what the group or organization stands for, have decided that its goals are your goals, and have determined where your particular skills and talents would be most useful. You then proceed to work for the cause, employing your particular strengths in its behalf.

Full commitment involves reasoned rather than emotional choices. It deals with logic rather than misplaced loyalty. It's the antithesis of the Scatter Shot School of Social Responsibility.

The system I recommend comprises a series of preplanned steps. First, as soon as a request for service reaches you, stall. Unless you are certain beyond the shadow of a doubt that you're not interested in what's being outlined, or conversely, that this is precisely the opportunity you've been waiting for, ask for time to think it over. Twenty-four to forty-eight hours is a reasonable interval in which to make your decision.

With the time you've bought, launch a carefully structured questioning process. You've seen these questions before; they are the same questions that begin the delegation procedure. That's because, in this case, you're deciding whether or not to delegate to yourself. First ask yourself, "Is this job necessary?" A lot of what passes for work, particularly in the voluntary sector, is downright silly. My personal bête noire is nametags. Even though perfectly serviceable nametags are widely available, some poor schnook always gets stuck making "cutesy" ones. There are a good many comparable scut jobs that seem to fall into the category of "women's work." Not only are they unnecessary, they're insulting. Obviously, you don't have time for this kind of useless occupation, so if you decide the task is irrelevant, you can decline with thanks and not even a trace of guilt.

Should you determine that what you're being solicited for is necessary, a second question follows. "Why am I being asked to do this task?" Because they can't find anybody else? Because it's your turn? Because everybody knows you're a patsy? Or because you have some special talent in the required area? If you have a citywide reputation as a baker, it's logical for the auction committee of the Fund for the Terminally Tall to ask you to donate one of your cakes to the annual auction. Were you a welder, this request would make little sense. Find out why they especially want you.

The third question is the kicker. "Does this activity advance any of my own objectives?" Put more crassly, "What's in it for me?" I can't see your reaction to that question, but when I say it in seminars, I'm sometimes met with stunned silence. "What's in it for me?" is not something we've been taught to consider. Such a notion goes against the grain of women as "self-less" givers; the idea of gaining something for ourselves while helping others seems callous and calculating. It is neither. The third question isn't selfish; it's smart.

Where is it written that in order to help others you have to be miserable? Does suffering through a task you despise somehow make the finished product more noble? Is your time so much less valuable than others' that you can afford to waste it in activities that bore you? Do you not work better when there is a possibility of reward for your labors?

The "what's in it for me" reward doesn't have to be monetary. If one of your objectives is to meet ten new people, the opportunity to work on a project with a whole range of people you've never seen before may be your payoff. Maybe you plan to go back to work as a counselor; your invitation to serve as a sounding board for the high school student council might be just what you need to get your skills honed. Perhaps, within a few years, you'd like to have a substantial say in how heart research money is spent in your community. Hiking up and down your street as a canvasser can get your foot in the door of the local Heart Association. By working "up the chairs" for a while, you can arrive at the decision-making stage fairly quickly. Even the most menial tasks can lead you where you want to go. Sometimes a job that looks dumb on the surface is the entry point to a whole new life. But beware. Sometimes a job that looks dumb on the surface is dumb all the way through. Choose with care. And put aside any guilt you may feel about doing well while doing good. The only thing you've done by making a choice in your own behalf is to ensure some personal growth at the same time you're serving others. That kind of decision requires no justification.

By now, you have a handle on your perception of the job as a whole. At this point, you need to check the accuracy of that perception. You can stop asking yourself questions for a time and get down to specific issues with those who seek your services. What is the job description? Is it short or long term? Are you being asked to create a project out of whole cloth or simply to follow a "cookbook" procedure? Will it require great blocks of time at intermittent intervals or a nearly constant level of activity over the life of the project?

With this information in hand, you require one more answer of yourself. Given the fact that you want to carry out this assignment, do you have sufficient reserves of time and energy to give to it? Can you engage yourself fully or will full commitment lead to burn-out? You cannot do everything. No matter how many worthy causes you immerse yourself in, there will always be one more. Many of them will be things you care deeply about, but choices will have to be made.

Whatever choice you make—go or no go—this careful investigation produces better decisions. You'll find a greater measure of satisfaction with your judgments when you consider your own needs as well as others'. Service you give to others because you've been coerced is service grudgingly given—and that's bad service.

Caring that includes some consideration for your strengths and knowledge of your limitations is caring you can enter into wholly. It is caring that comes from the heart. Which would you rather offer?

EXERCISE 14:

Consider carefully all your affiliations and organizations. Determine both what you're giving and what you're getting from your membership in these groups. Take whatever action you feel is appropriate regarding those you've outgrown or simply don't like anymore. (I know a woman who once wrote twelve letters of resignation in one day. She'd felt she was advancing her husband's career by her membership in various organizations. When he told her that he didn't need that kind of help—and never had—her relief was unbounded and her pen very busy!)

SECTION 3

DAYS 15–21

*in which you discover
that the first two
sections didn't have
all the answers*

DAY 15

More Help for the Fritters

Well, it's back in the saddle again with the time logs. Start filling one out today and continue through Day 21. Now that you're aware of your goals, objectives, and plans, know something about Pareto and his principle, and have analyzed your areas of time misuse, this set of logs will reflect the new-you-on-the-way. You're not the same person you were two weeks ago. You've grown and changed, and your time sheets will show it.

To make sure that you keep plugging away on your record keeping, I've designed very simple readings for the rest of the week, and there'll be no daily exercises besides making your log entries. For the next few days, we'll be dealing with the most commonly asked questions concerning the WOMANHOURS system. Today's questions center on frittering.

Q. I think you're pretty callous. "If you don't have time for people, say so." What am I supposed to do with a friend who needs help—tell her to bug off and come back when I feel like dealing with her problems?

A. If you thought I was callous before, you're really going to be appalled now. The answer to your question is, it depends. Obviously, an actual emergency requires immediate attention. Has something catastrophic happened? Is your friend a potential suicide? Has she or a member of her family had an accident or suddenly been taken ill? Is she grieving over the loss of loved ones through death or divorce? Has she been fired or suffered any other major dislocation? Then drop everything and go to her. That's what friends are for.

Some people, though, are professional "leaners." They use up their friends, manufacturing crises at every opportunity. They rehash the same woeful tales day after day, week after week. Should you find yourself listening to yet another repetition of the same theme and variations, back off. You're doing your friend no favor by providing an audience for her histrionics.

You may, in fact, be doing her harm. As she rants and raves to you, she's consuming energy that could better be spent in coping with the reality of her situation, whatever it is. By constantly *talking* about her problem, she delays *doing* anything about it, and by listening to her, you become her accomplice.

I'm not saying you should never try to help a Calamity Jane, but get out of the picture when your instincts tell you you're being used. When your stomach knots up at the sound of her voice; when you stop answering your phone because you fear she's on the other end of the line, the relationship has become destructive to you. No definition of friendship includes the right of one friend to usurp the total life of the other.

Q. I'm a dental assistant, and my biggest problem is salespeople. I can't get anything done because these people make drop-in calls. They all have new products; some of them are exciting and my boss might be interested in them, but this way of doing business is messing up my day's schedule a lot.

A. Wait a minute! Who's in charge here? It's *your* office and these people are trying to sell *you* a product. I would notify each company that salespeople will be seen by appointment only. There are various ways to structure these visits. Perhaps you'd like to deal with all the sales reps one day a month on a first-come, first-seen basis. Maybe you'd prefer individual appointments at regularly scheduled intervals. Whatever you decide, there is *no* reason to be at the mercy of drop-ins.

You may have to sell the salespeople on this idea, but that should be a snap. Point out to them that if they have an appointment, they're assured of your full attention. Undistracted by other matters, you can concentrate exclusively on their products and information. Surely most salespeople would prefer to call on a relaxed, receptive client. And if they won't buy your system, they won't sell much in your office. You're in the driver's seat. Drive!

Q. Speaking of driving, the most serious time waster I have is chauffeuring my kids. We live in the suburbs, and it's a couple of miles to everything! I hate to restrict their activities just because the constant driving is such a pain.

A. I can identify with you. Until my son received his driver's license, I felt that my car and I were one, that I was more intimately involved with its machinery than with my husband. When the car burped, the whole family went into shock.

The alternatives to continual driving are, of course, car pools (usually more of a hassle than they're worth), bicycles (if the kids are old enough and the streets dry enough), public transportation (if available in your area), and walking. I favor walking. My daughter's kindergarten teacher asked that parents not drive the kids to school, but let them walk—in rain, snow, sun, wind—to get a sense of the natural world and a feeling of their own strength. Since she's in her seventies and still climbing mountains, I think she was on to something. A properly outfitted kid isn't going to be hurt by a little rain or snow.

Children can be hurt by other people, though, so I advocate their traveling in a group.

I also recommend taking a long, hard look at your kids' activities. Are they all things the children enjoy, or are some of them simply "everyone does it" operations? Are you pushing your child into baseball, ballet, baton twirling, or bassoon lessons, so that he or she will be "well rounded?" Some of the "roundest" kids have ulcers and other stress-related problems. How much of what you're complaining about have you brought on yourself by wanting your child to have "every opportunity"? Feel it out with your kids. They may not like hopping around at the Junior Dancing Assembly any more than you like driving them there every week. Take them— and yourself—off the hook.

Last, you might consider moving. I know that's a drastic option, but how much do you dislike driving? Closer to the city means more public transportation, shorter distances to travel, and a wider range of cultural and social opportunities. Suburbs offer cleaner air, greener grass, quieter neighborhoods—and driving. It's a trade-off. How does your family want to play it?

Q. My greatest fritter wasn't even mentioned in the chapter. It's meetings! I spend over 40 percent of my work time in meetings, and most of them are useless.

A. That's a dreadful waste of womanhours. I would begin immediately to document every minute I've spent in meetings and identify what results my attendance had for my department. With this documentation, I'd march in to my supervisor and see what suggestions he or she has to alleviate this ridiculous situation.

If you're told to stop rocking the boat—that meeting attendance is required—I'd suggest that you go only for that portion of the meeting that deals directly with issues relevant to your department. Try this idea out on your boss before you skip a meeting. If he or she is agreeable, then get an advance agenda, so you can plan when to come and go.

I'd also look at the possibility of rotating the responsibility for attendance around your division or section. Surely there's someone else who can represent the department.

At the meetings themselves, be active. Discover the purpose of the meeting at the outset, and help keep the discussion on track. Assist the chairperson in holding to the agenda. If debate has become repetitive, summarize it and call the question. Don't be afraid to be assertive; the others will probably bless your name.

Should all else fail, treat useless meetings as time off. Plan your wardrobe, make out your grocery list, jot down tomorrow's to-do list, write your mother. You can always read the minutes of the meeting later to find out what happened. (Probably nothing.)

Q. My meetings are of a volunteer organization, but they're just as bad. What's the solution?

A. The same as above. Volunteers are much too scarce and valuable to have their time wasted in unproductive meetings. Learn all you can about effective meetings and help your chairperson structure them. If you can't get anywhere, resign. Find an organization that treats volunteers with respect. In volunteer work, the pay's the same whether you show up or not. Your reward comes in the quality of your service. Seek out an agency that knows how to work with volunteers and support it. Don't bother with those who devalue your gift of time.

Q. My problem has to do with the telephone. Once I get on, I can't seem to get off. Can you give me some tactful turnoffs?

A. The simplest way to get off the phone is to set up the end of the conversation at the beginning. When I was growing up, my family had a code phrase. When one of us called the other, and the "callee" was rushed, she said, "What can I do for you?" (I was later surprised to find that Edwin C. Bliss recommended the identical phrase for the identical reason in his book, *Getting Things Done.* I had no idea my family were such good managers!) Equally effective phrases are "How can I help you?" or "What do you need?" If the caller indicates that it's just a social jingle, you're free to say you're tied up and will call back. If it's a matter that can be dispatched quickly, "What can I do for you?" gets all the cards out on the table right away. You settle the issue, exchange a pleasantry or two, and hang up.

If I'm stuck with a droner, I find myself saying, "Goodness, I didn't mean to keep you all morning. I'm sure you have things to do. I'll talk to you soon." It's very graceful—and very effective.

Of course, you can always fall back on the old "someone at the door" dodge, but that's pretty transparent. Everybody does it.

The most creative (and devious) call-ending technique I've heard of involves hanging up while *you're* talking and then taking your phone off the hook. The caller will think you've been disconnected. When she redials, she'll get a busy signal, assume you have trouble on your line, and give up (or kindly report your problem to the phone company). I'd save this one for dire emergencies.

In general, tactful honesty is still the best policy.

Q. I've found that the biggest help to me is a "call-waiting" option on my telephone. With it, I can chat with a friend and never miss an important call. Why don't you recommend this to your clients?

A. Because for me, "call-waiting" was an unmitigated disaster. I tried it for a month, but had it removed after one ghastly afternoon when I took a daisy chain of calls that lasted for four solid hours. The memory of that afternoon is etched forever in my brain. It gave me a cauliflower ear, an intensive-care headache, and a fierce determination never to make myself that available again.

Innovation does not necessarily mean progress!

Q. I'd like to try the telephone hour idea, but I'm afraid my friends will be offended. It sounds as if I'm saying that I'm more important than they are. Won't they think I'm getting arrogant?

A. Not if they're real friends. Real friends—those who understand that friendship means caring for one another—will applaud your decision to unscramble your life.

They'll also discover, paradoxical as it sounds, that decreasing your availability increases your approachability. When they call you after you've instituted your new regimen, they'll find that you're less preoccupied, less frustrated, less vexed. You'll have the time to be fully involved with them and their concerns. By protecting yourself, you'll improve the quality of the relationship.

It's possible, however, that there will be acquaintances who'll be put off by your telephone hours. Unless the caller is your brain surgeon, a Mafia don, or Robert Redford, I'd ignore any disapproval. After all, "Sticks and stones, etc."

Q. I don't understand your emphasis on concentration. What's the value of doing one thing at a time? All the time management books I've ever read tell me to do two jobs at once.

A. I know. I've seen those books too. And, of course, doing two things at once makes sense in certain cases. Mindless tasks can certainly be done two at a time. Manicure your nails while watching TV. Exercise while talking on the phone. Run the washer while you're stirring the soup. Those kinds of duos are possible and timesaving.

But there are jobs that can't be combined. You can't bake a birthday cake while you're typing a report. You can't clean the basement at the same time you're practicing a Beethoven sonata. It's highly unlikely that you can hem Sara's dresses while you change the spark plugs in the Jeep. The most efficient way to complete all these diverse tasks is to concentrate fully on one at a time—in an orderly sequence—until they're all done. Dashing back and forth from one to the other, even in thought, is inefficient, time-wasting behavior. An efficient person is one who has learned the habit of discipline, and discipline begins in the mind.

Q. Don't you think St. Theresa's Little Way could lead to perfectionism, though?

A. I suppose it could, but it's more likely that it will simply teach you to see a task through to completion before starting another. The Little Way is a meditation. Perfectionism can be circumvented by another meditation—by chanting as your mantra, "Never do a job better than it needs to be done." Get out the incense, ladies. You too can learn to be less than perfect.

EXERCISE 15:

START A NEW TIME LOG. I HEAR YOU MOANING, BUT IT'S GOOD FOR YOU.

DAY 16

Dandy Delegation: Part 2

The questions and answers today deal with failure to delegate.

Q. Your discussion about delegation seemed to deal mainly with the office. I'm a homemaker. My kids are old enough to help out. How do delegation methods work with kids?

A. The same way they work with adults. The age of the children determines the kind of discussion you have with them, but the techniques remain the same.

Because so much of what is delegated around the house is scut work, it's particularly important that results be the standard of performance. To a kid, it's bad enough that he has to do the ironing in the first place. It's worse if he has to put up with Mom hanging over his shoulder, criticizing his methods. ("Where did you learn to press a shirt like *that?* You do it like *this!*) Remember, once you've taught the job, stand back and let your delegate perform. Allow for deviations and style differences. Unless it's dangerous, the method of operation is supremely unimportant if the agreed-upon results are achieved.

I speak with some authority here because I messed up delegation so badly with my own kids. When they first became responsible for after-dinner KP, I stood in the kitchen each evening, shrieking because they did this, that, and the other thing "wrong." The postdinner hour became so unpleasant that I finally got smart and hung up a four-by-six-inch card that listed the specifications for an acceptable job. Taped on the refrigerator door, the "spec sheet" read: The kitchen is clean when: (1) All dishes are in dishwasher, pots and pans are scrubbed and put away; (2) all counters are scrubbed; (3) fronts of all equipment are wiped down; (4) all food is replaced in cupboards or refrigerator; (5) the sink is scoured; (6) the floor is swept; (7) the lights are out.

The sign was my representative. When the kids thought the job was done, they consulted the "specs," not me. For a short while, I made an inspection tour each evening to double-check results. I was able to give that part up quickly, though, as the children became both proficient and responsible.

Kids are creative. I know one little girl who drags sofa cushions onto the floor and vacuums them. To her it's a lot simpler than fiddling around with the attachments. Her mother says it doesn't hurt the couch, and it's faster and more thorough than a whisk broom. I also know a young man who won't iron shirttails. He's aware of the belt line. Below that, forget it—and why not?

I'm sure you could cite similar examples. Rather than bellow at kids for their unorthodox methods, let's marvel at the unfettered imaginations that conjure up such inventive problem-solving techniques.

Q. I understand the emphasis on results, but how did you convince your kids to take KP in the first place? Every time I make a suggestion, all I get is a lot of complaining and back talk.

A. Of course! So did I. It isn't going to be all sweetness and light. At least it wasn't around my house. What I did, though, was appeal to the kids' sense of justice. If you've ever listened to children argue, you've noticed how concerned they are with what's "fair." Though we've explained to our children repeatedly that in the larger sense, life very often isn't fair (men of peace are assassinated while terrorists flourish; kind people suffer debilitating illness; virtuous people struggle while the J. R. Ewings of this world prosper, etc.), it is still our responsibility to be just in our daily lives. Against this ethical backdrop, it was easy to work with them.

    I pointed out to them that I fixed the dinner every night while they played or did homework or watched television. They came to the table, ate, and enjoyed the meal and returned to their pursuits while I remained in the kitchen until after 8:00 P.M. Since they were both able bodied, was this a just situation? When did I have time for a quiet conversation with their father or just a chance to sit down? I didn't whine or play "poor little me." I just stated the facts. They bought it—slowly and grudgingly to be sure—but they bought it. They made up their own rules for duty nights, substitutions, and other details, and we were on our way.

Q. My delegation to my kids started that way, but they resisted at the beginning, and they kept on resisting. We started fighting all the time. Finally I gave up. It was easier to keep the peace and do it all myself.

A. Easier for whom? If you asked my advice (and I think you just did), I'd recommend that you examine your delegation process and start again.

    Why did your children resist? Did you delegate real jobs

or make-work? Were your standards of performance initially too high? Did you delineate clearly the expected results? Did you teach the job or expect the kids to pick it up by osmosis? Even the simplest task is fraught with pitfalls for the child who's never tried it before. Did you delegate to the right child? Your five-feet-eight-inch daughter may be better equipped for heavy outdoor work than her five-feet-two older brother, to whom you might unthinkingly assign such tasks. Sex-linked delegation is out! Did you give your delegate freedom to roam around in the job, discovering alternate ways to accomplish the results? Did you listen to the kids' suggestions and questions?

You did? And it still didn't work? Then the problem is in your attitude. Though it's understandable that you caved into the need for your children's approval (women are often notorious approval seekers), steel yourself not to do so again.

Unless they have specific, reasonable, and correctable grievances, turn a deaf ear to the kids' bellyaching. Their disapproval is only unpleasant, not life threatening. Recognize that a few intrafamily squabbles are normal. Keep your sense of humor; a well-timed laugh can defuse many an explosive situation. Empathize copiously—and don't give an inch.

Q. Things were so far gone at our house that I couldn't get anybody even to discuss a division of labor, let alone act on it. So I went on strike. What do you think of this as a tactic?

A. I think it's terrific. I did it myself once for an entire week, and as you indicate, it's a real attention grabber. The only thing I did for that week was cook. There was no laundry service, no chauffeur service, no errand running, no housecleaning. It was very difficult to do. The kids hated it. They were angry, confused, and frustrated. They complained to their friends, who complained to their parents—who cheered!

Even with the support of the other parents, though, it was a rough week, and in the end everyone—including the striker—was ready for a negotiated settlement.

Drastic situations call for drastic measures. If things are really out of hand at your house, a strike might be useful. Prepare yourself for rampant disapproval.

Q. My kids are too little to be any help, and I'm a single parent. I can't afford a maid or cleaning service. To whom do I delegate?

A. You're really in a tough situation, but it's not hopeless. With your budget crunch, I'd look into barter. Are there teenagers in your neighborhood who would exchange a few hours' housework for the chance to practice on your piano or use your typewriter or get some help with their math? Talk to the guidance office or the principal of your local high school.

Another possibility is a women's barter network. Are you good at cooking, baking, tailoring, accounting, wallpapering, landscaping, party planning, package wrapping, auto mechanics, bargain hunting? All these abilities are in demand. Talk to your friends. Exchange hateful jobs. Balancing a checkbook might be anathema to a domestically oriented neighbor, but duck soup for you. Balance the checkbook for her in exchange for some housecleaning. It's not as far out as it might seem. Groups like this exist around the country. If there's none in your area, start one.

A third option is to find a friend or two and work as a housecleaning team. Three or four people working together can whiz through the average house or apartment very quickly. For deep-down cleaning, once every couple of weeks is enough.

Money is never the only medium of exchange. Be inventive. What can you trade for time?

Q. You're very hard on kids and friends and very easy on husbands. Where does dear old Dad fit into the delegation picture?

A. You're right. I've been avoiding this issue, because it's difficult for me. The only marriage with which I'm intimately acquainted (mine) is a very traditional one. Though extraordinarily liberated in many respects, my husband is unreconstructed in his view that men don't do housework. I've been plugging away on this issue for almost twenty years; I think it's unlikely that I shall overcome. For family feasts and parties, he'll get in there and pitch, but daily work is definitely "woman's work." My particular blessing is that he isn't fussy about *what* woman does the work, so he was agreeable to my hiring some day help who happened to be female.

He's happy, I'm happy, and Maude, my helper, is happy, so it's worked out very well.

I recognize, though, that this option isn't available for everyone, and in traditional families, housework is the hardest nut to crack.

It's possible that you'll be able to effect a change in dear old Dad (providing that he really is a dear old Dad) by reminding him that he's doing a disservice to both his sons and daughters by modeling behavior that will be inappropriate by the time his children are grown.

A boy who grows up expecting to be catered to will have trouble relating to women; a girl who learns to wait passively for some guy to take care of everything outside the house will be in for a shock. The institution of marriage is changing, and even the most traditional families need to prepare their children.

In homes where both spouses have outside occupations,

in-house division of labor should be a given. Unfortunately latest studies tell us that men are still assiduously avoiding carrying their share of the load. It's no wonder; women have been griping about housework forever. Why would any sane, sensible man want to take it on?

Whether he *wants* to do his part isn't the issue, however, The issue is whether or not you're satisfied to be a packhorse.

If working two full-time jobs isn't your idea of fun, say so. Your husband is not a clairvoyant. I'm continually surprised by the number of women who martyr it out and expect mind reading to be part of their husband's bag of tricks. When it isn't, the wives berate their mates for being "insensitive" and "unfeeling." It's a bum rap; he's just ignorant. Wise him up and see what happens.

When nothing happens, put it to him in economic terms. Tell him that from now on, part of the family earnings will go toward household help. Faced with a reduction in your purchasing power, your husband may see the light posthaste. Money still talks. In the event that he doesn't start to negotiate, hire the help. You deserve it, you need it, and you should have it.

Q. What if the person I delegate to really screws up the job?

A. That shouldn't happen if you've taught the task thoroughly, have adequate feedback mechanisms, and personally inspect the situation from time to time.

If your delegate really blows it, I'm afraid that you have to bear some of the responsibility, unless he or she is a total dunce. (And in that case, why did you select him or her for the job in the first place?)

Q. When I do a job, I know it will be done right, and having things done properly is important to me. What do I do about delegating?

A. It seems to me that you're saying two things. One is that you want good results. The other is that you want things done your way—and only your way. The first is possible through delegation. The second is not. The authority to do the task must go with the delegation; you can't have it both ways. Until you resolve this conflict, what you do about delegating is nothing.

Q. The part about fear of subordinates' success really got to me. I'm scared to death I'll delegate myself out of work.

A. You probably will—right into a promotion. I think you're dealing with a phantom fear. As you become a successful delegator, it's likely that you'll be seen as management material, because your department will be productive and your bottom line outstanding. Chance it!

EXERCISE 16:

KEEP UP THE TIME LOG HABIT.

DAY 17
Finishing Off Filling In

Today's questions and answers will give you more information about filling in.

Q. I think the Pareto Principle is very interesting. What happens, though, if the tasks you think are of most value don't coincide with someone else's estimate of what's valuable for you? I like to run a couple of miles every morning before work. My husband feels that I should spend that time with him while he eats breakfast. I'd like to compromise, but I'm at my best in the morning, my time is limited, and that's when I want to run.

A. A situation such as you describe is sometimes called a "values collision." Though I don't think your circumstances are beyond remedy, values collisions can be very difficult to resolve.

In your case, physical fitness is obviously one of your life goals. It sounds as if physical closeness is one of your husband's. Since you're both employed and lead busy lives, it makes sense that he'd want to touch base with you before the work day begins and you go your separate ways. It also makes sense for you to perform a high-value routine while you're at a high-energy level.

You don't say what kind of compromises you've offered. I assume, though, that you've already tried to get your husband to run with you. That, of course, would be ideal; you'd get your exercise and he'd get his conversation.

Life is rarely ideal, however, so failing that idea, you could begin your run fifteen minutes earlier in the morning. That should get you back in time to have a glass of juice while he finishes his eggs.

Perhaps mornings just aren't possible. Try midday instead. Make a lunch date with your husband several times a week, |o r, at the least, give him a call during your lunch hour. Both of you could brown-bag the midday meal and have long-distance lunch together.

Brainstorm as a couple. I'm sure you can come up with many solutions, so long as neither one of you plants your feet too firmly. There are values collisions that aren't so amenable to solutions, however. These occur when one partner holds a full-blown set of beliefs about how the other "should" think, feel, and behave. To ameliorate the conflict these unrealistic expectations can generate, I recommend that both partners participate in a task-stripping exercise together.

See what the essence of your values collisons is. Once you know, the two of you can converse, compromise, conciliate—as a team. Or you can find a mediator. However you decide to proceed, your relationship is worth working on.

Q. Does the Pareto Principle have applications other than to time management?

A. Yes, Vilfredo Pareto was a nineteenth-century economist, so it's not surprising that you can make his principle apply to situations dealing with money.

Suppose, for example, that you discover that 80 percent of your food dollar is spent on meat and processed convenience items—which constitute about 20 percent of your total grocery purchase. That's an eye-opener. Research has shown that we'd all be better off with a diet richer in fiber and complex carbohydrates and lower in fats, salt, and sugar. Meats and expensive processed foods have a much smaller role to play in such a regimen, so if you're interested in a new and healthier food choice, you'll immediately reorder your spending habits. Some of the meat money could be shifted to buy top-of-the-line produce and whole grain products. You'd certainly be getting more for less—and a much greater percentage of your money would be spent on higher-priority items.

As was mentioned in the discussion of Pareto, another area of money misuse is clothing. Though it's best to buy quality for daily wear and to conserve money on clothes rarely worn, some women act as if the opposite were true. How many of you have most of your clothing budget tied up in garments you wear 20 percent of the time or less—while you scrimp, save, and stretch the budget for the skirts, pants, shirts, and jackets that are your wardrobe essentials?

Considering any purchase from a value-received as well as a dollar-cost angle will help you make better buying decisions, whether the item purchased is a garlic press or an airplane.

Q. My question is about list making. I like a long to-do list. It's satisfying to check off all the tasks as I do them. Why should I change?

A. I agree that there's something very gratifying about crossing off a long list of completed projects. It can provide a real feeling of accomplishment. But a list like that can be a trap as well. Is your list composed of low-value, two-bit tasks that you're performing just so you can check them off? Many women hide behind such a list. Afraid of risk and growth, they use their lists as a crutch to show others how "busy" they are. They couldn't possibly accept a new or challenging assignment: their to-do list is much too crowded as it is. Though it may not be true in your case, a long list can be an invitation to infantilism.

Q. Why all this talk about list making in the first place? I take life one day at a time and do what has to be done that day. Worrying about goals and plans for tomorrow is useless. There may not be a tomorrow. I'm getting along fine with my family and friends with no plans and no lists at all.

A. Congratulations! You must have an incredible memory. You also have a real grasp of an important truth. Today is all we have. Worrying about tomorrow is indeed pointless, and devaluing today while looking forward to future rewards is just plain silly. We must learn to revel in our present moments.

There's a distinction, though, between "futurizing" and planning for the future. I think forward planning is essential. A woman who has no life plan will flounder for an inordinate length of time should her support network of friends and family be undercut. Ask any displaced homemaker whether she'd have been better off with some future planning. It's mandatory that we develop strategies that depend on our own attributes and capabilities, not someone else's.

What has a list to do with all this? A daily list, headed by a statement of the day's objectives, keeps your vision of your life plan fresh. It's no big deal to toss a life plan together; the trick is nurturing it after its birth. A to-do list helps.

So while I agree with you that present moments are all we're sure of, spending them carelessly is not the most effective way to live.

Q. I procrastinate, and I think I'm doing it to create excitement. What alternative do you suggest?

A. The list of ways to engender positive excitement is endless.

What do you like to do? Are you interested in art? Reward yourself before, during, and after a difficult task with a trip to an unfamiliar gallery, a print for the living room, an art appreciation seminar. Sketch the skyline on your lunch hour. Visit a studio. Meet an artist. Feed your curiosity and originality.

What have you always wanted? To dance with a ballet company? Maybe you can't do that now, but you can keep up your interest in ballet. Rev yourself up for other projects by nourishing your ballet lover side. Purchase season tickets. Subscribe to a dance magazine. Attend the local dancing school's annual recital; the three- and four-year-old ballerinas are worth the price of the gas. Collect a series of dance posters; decorate the bathroom with them. Do whatever keeps you in touch with your unique and singular dreams.

Reach deep down into yourself. Invite the spontaneous, childlike part of you out to play. Ask her what she'd like to do. Kids are always excited about something; the child-in-you is no different. If you give that special child some freedom, the adult self can settle down, and your work habits will likely improve.

Q. I procrastinate at the end of a job I've enjoyed because I don't want it to end. Right now I'm putting off the completion of redecorating my house. Are you suggesting that I need a psychiatrist because I'm "denying [myself] the satisfaction a completed project would bring"? I don 't think I'm sick.

A. Of course you're not sick. What you're describing is the conscious prolongation of an enjoyable task or relationship, not an unconscious desire to punish yourself. Perhaps you can find similar jobs, and, of course, the end of a project doesn't have to mean the end of relationships. Make a special effort to see those people you've come to value. Don't just exchange platitudes about having lunch sometime. Make some definite plans now—and stick to them. That should ease the pain of task termination.

Q. Have you ever seen that plaque that says, "Housework is something nobody notices until you stop doing it?" That's me. I put off the housework because that's the only way I get noticed. I'm the original invisible woman. As you mentioned, even negative attention is better than none. When I let the house go to pot, somebody finally realizes that I'm around, even if the feedback is all rotten. I hate myself for behaving this way, but I'm fed up with being ignored. How else can I get my husband and family to notice my existence?

A. First, stop hating yourself immediately! Self-hatred accomplishes nothing and uses up energy you need to drag yourself out of your despondency. Second, congratulate yourself for making such an honest, courageous analysis of your life situation. It takes real guts to admit that you're behaving in a self-destructive manner. It takes even more guts to ask for help. Third, recognize that your family treats you like the old crone who comes in to clean the toilets because you allow them to do so. Investigate why you perpetuate this state of affairs. Last, acknowledge that you're a person of worth and value even if nobody else feeds that opinion back to you. You're obviously a woman with ferocious will power. You have to be, to procrastinate so well for such long periods of time. Unleash that will power in your own behalf. Develop some aspect of yourself that you've neglected. Cultivate new interests and new people. Take pleasure in your growth. If no one else is noticing you, *you* notice you. I guarantee that as you become more interested in yourself, other people will begin to take interest as well.

And, for heaven's sake, get that family of yours involved in doing their share around the house!

Q. I've tried several methods to stop my procrastination, and I'm getting better about it. Do you have any quick and easy formula that might be useful when I just need a swift kick to get me off my duff?

A. I don't know if it's a formula, but when I need some impetus, I ask a question I picked up from Wayne Dyer's *Your Erroneous Zones*. The question is, "What's the worst thing that will happen if I do this job?" Notice that the question doesn't ask what will occur if I *don't* act. I already know those consequences, and usually they're too depressing to contemplate. My question is much more encouraging. Since the outcome of completing a task is almost always positive, even the worst that could happen will still be pretty good. I find that this talisman sentence motivates me quickly.

Q. What do you think of setting deadlines as an antiprocrastination device?

A. In general, I think deadlines are overrated. I admit that they have some value for those who have trouble finishing an assignment. I question their utility, however, in assisting people who have difficulty beginning a task. That's always been my problem, and I suspect I could gather an army of similar sufferers—if I could get them to show up on time.

EXERCISE 17:

TIME LOG!

DAY 18

Some More Rest for the Weary

Tired? The questions and answers featured today may show you why.

Q. I think I'm so tired because I'm so bored all the time. What do you suggest for me?

A. I'm sorry to say you've just pressed one of my buttons. Unless she is recuperating from a long illness, there is no reason for any woman in this country to be bored. Though short bouts of occasional ennui may be unavoidable, a woman who says she's constantly bored will get very little sympathy from me. There are too many questions that need answering, too much music that needs hearing, too many books that need reading, too many hands that need holding for anyone to say she has nothing to do. Your local volunteer action center will be overjoyed to welcome you. There are people and institutions crying for help. Search them out. Read to the blind, comfort the dying, escort kids through the zoo, take your turn at Suicide Prevention, become a docent at the museum. Crawl out of your cave, lady, and get busy.

If it's your job that bores you—and there's no possibility of leaving it—develop an avocation that challenges you.

Occasionally, boredom is a mask for depression. In that case, all the above advice still goes. Making a life beyond your misery is one of the keys to relieving a low mood.

A little love, a little service to others will breathe new vitality into your life—and into you. Remember, a bored woman is a boring woman.

Q. I have a daytime job, but I'm not really alert until about noon. My morning hours are just sleepwalking. I've thought about a night job, but my husband works days, and we'd never see each other. Is there an answer for me?

A. I think you have at least a couple of options. First consider flextime. It might be possible for you to arrive at work a couple of hours later in the morning and remain later in the afternoon. Your employer would certainly benefit from your heightened productivity. You'd gain a couple of hours of low-energy time to handle routine tasks at home, you'd drive to work when you're more alert (less chance of accidents and resultant sick leave!), and you'd avoid rush hour going home. Maybe you could convince your boss to make you part of a flextime pilot project. It's worth a try.

My other recommendation would be to investigate job sharing. This isn't a possibility if you must have full-time employment, but it can be an original and satisfying way to work part time.

Two job sharers can arrange their tasks and hours variously. Each duo has its own style. Sometimes one partner is on a week, then off a week. Other women split the week. In your case, it sounds as if you'd do well to find a partner to handle things in the morning, while you take the afternoon shift.

Job sharing requires coordination, cooperation, and organization, but it can be instituted in almost any situation—office, lab, school, or shop.

The advantages to you are that you're in the office only during your peak hours, and you and your partner may be able to split the benefits package of one full-time job. The disadvantage is that if you are considered a part-time employee, your benefits are reduced if they exist at all. Be prudent, but keep an open mind.

Q. I'm a morning person like you. I have two toddlers and would like to use my prime time to do the high-quality mothering I know I'm capable of. But just as you described, I'm wasting hours mopping up the mess after breakfast, picking up the toys, running a load of wash every morning, and so on. These chores just have to be done; otherwise I'll be up to my hips in dirt and clutter in no time. The problem is, by the time I finish making order out of chaos every morning, I'm too annoyed, crabby, and resentful to be much of a mom. My mothering is defintely third-class. I love my kids, but sometimes I could scream!

A. I can understand that. My kids are teenagers now, but I remember—oh boy, do I remember!

Your problem is that you're all tied up in the American Puritan work ethic, which holds that work must precede pleasure. Before you can read to the kids or take them on an outing or accompany them to the backyard to observe ants, the dishes *must* be done, the clothes *must* be washed, the house *must* be picked up.

This is sheer baloney, and your question shows that you know it. I think you're just looking for permission to alter your work style. You've got it. Let the dishes soak until afternoon, toss the laundry in before naptime, "deshamble-ize" the house no more than once a day (and get Dad and the kids involved). Experiment with new times for old jobs. There's nothing sacred about your present routine if it doesn't meet your needs. A routine should free you up; when it constrains you, it's time to renovate it.

By the way, in that overhauled routine, be sure to include some time just for you. No matter how adorable the tots, two under three will wear you down. As you take better care of yourself, your resentment ratio will fall.

Q. I work days, go to school three nights a week, and have custody of my daughter. I'm exhausted. What now?

A. Obviously, you can't quit your job if you and your daughter want to continue eating. But for you, too, flextime might be useful. As little as an hour's more sleep in the morning could probably pep you up.

I assume that your educational endeavors are directed toward career advancement. Unless there's a promotion deadline or the like, you might consider extending your deadline for the completion of your program. If you can set back your date only a semester or quarter, you'll take a load off your shoulders. I know that kind of delay often doesn't seem like a real option, but take a second look at it. You're talking about stopping out for about ten to twelve weeks. Considering the larger picture, will that brief time make a real difference in achieving your goals? Is the present threat to your physical and emotional health great enough to consider such a delay? Would you be better off regaining some equilibrium now? I'm not suggesting that you quit forever, but that you take a brief hiatus. I've done it; I managed to cram four years of college into five, and I think it was a good decision.

I hope your custody arrangements allow you some time on the weekends to use for your personal refreshment and recreation. Part of your fatigue stems from the sameness of your days. Break the pattern and your energy level should rebound, at least to some extent.

Q. I'm a housewife. My prime time is between 2:00 to 6:00 A.M. Am I supposed to leap out of bed and do my dusting and vacuuming then? It seems a little weird to me.

A. First of all, you're not "supposed" to do anything. But if, in fact, 2:00-6:00 A.M. is your prime time, it seems a shame to lie awake wasting it. I wouldn't spend those peak hours dusting and vacuuming, though; those are low-energy tasks. Instead, I'd determine what I consider to be my most creative, demanding household work, and I'd reserve it for those hours. Bake bread, quilt, revamp your budget. You'll need to watch your noise level, but that should be your only consideration.

　　As to whether or not such behavior is weird, what do you care? Weird to whom? If it works for you, why should you care what the neighbors think? It's none of their business anyway. Live conveniently, not conventionally!

EXERCISE 18:

HAVE YOU KEPT YOUR LOG TODAY?

DAY 19

Your Last Fracas with Frazzle

Women who are frazzled may find some solutions in the questions and answers that follow. Though this is a very short chapter, containing only a few questions, they're the ones that come up again and again.

Q. Your exercise for Day 14 is irresponsible. Are you suggesting that we should just drop out? What if we have commitments to people who are counting on us?

A. I'm as compulsive as the next person and so would never advise that someone run out on her commitments to people and organizations. Given no extraordinary circumstances, you may have to see your committee chairmanship through to the bitter end, or continue at the helm of the fund-raising effort until the last dime is in the till.

But it's a rare woman who holds major responsibilities in every organization to which she belongs. You could bail out of many of them with scarcely a ripple. The only thing hurt in a situation like this is your ego, when you notice how quickly the remaining group members fill your vacant slot. It disabuses you of any notion of your indispensability.

You can sense almost immediately if you and a group are a good match. Are you both giving and getting from the group or is the group sucking you dry? Do you feel real satisfaction with your contributions or are you just pleasing someone else with your participation? Are you in sync with the aims of the organization? When you're not, don't hesitate to resign.

I left an advisory board once after one meeting, not because the group wasn't representing a worthy cause, but because their organizational goals were not my goals. Perhaps I should have anticipated their viewpoint, but it was impossible to ascertain from the outside. I resigned from another association after the second meeting because it was juvenile. Individual group members were women I didn't consider childish, but when they all got together in a meeting, it was like Romper Room on a rainy morning.

My speedy resignations did no damage to my credibility; my "flake factor" rating didn't soar out of sight. As a matter of fact, very few people were aware of my leave taking.

Since there are so many agencies, professional societies, schools and churches that need help, it's senseless to allow a group in which you're a halfhearted member to slurp up your time. Conserve your efforts, pick your spot, and make your contribution count.

Q. I'm required to join certain organizations as a condition of employment. My boss says I have to! So your method for choosing one's obligation is irrelevant to my situation.

A. Maybe yes, maybe no. If your boss wants you to join a trade association or professional society, he or she is doing you a favor. Women on the way up often complain that they're denied access to the informal communication network men are privy to. But if you keep your eyes and ears open, association gatherings can be gushers of information. A dinner meeting with a cash bar is sometimes a hotbed of gossip, with tidbits ranging from the sublime (who's leaving the job you've always coveted) to the ridiculous (the latest interoffice affair). I'd recommend that you attend such sessions and extend your antennae. Be active. Be visible. Be grateful to the boss who thinks enough of you to want you there.

Perhaps these kinds of memberships aren't the subject of your question, however. Does your boss want you on the board of a charity that bores you cross-eyed because it's his or her favorite? Have a candid chat with your employer. Explain, not that the charity bores you cross-eyed, but that you think the company could heighten its community visibility by allowing its employees to choose their own extracurriculars. Think what effective representation the corporation could have if its members fanned out all over the city, enthusiastically supporting their favorite causes, all the while maintaining their identities as associates of XYZ Insurance and Storm Door Sales, Ltd.

Since your boss values your opinion enough to want you to represent the company in public, he or she may listen to your suggestion. A boss who refuses to understand that you have a life beyond the office probably won't keep you very long.

Q. I don't have many outside activities, but I seem to get frazzled with things. I'm not rich, but nonetheless I'm drowning in possessions. There are so many objects in my life and my house, there's hardly room for me.

A. I understand what you're saying. Sometimes it seems that our belongings own us rather than the other way around. All these objects take maintenance, care, and storage space. Our life, if we're not careful, can be utilized almost completely on behalf of things.

Thoreau had the right idea—simplify, simplify. And remember, in every room of the house, 80 percent of the value of that room will come from 20 percent of the objects in it.

Let's look into your kitchen. Using Pareto's Principle, find the vital few utensils that provide most of the kitchen's value, and make sure they're accessible. Now fix your beady little eyes on the rest of the stuff you use for cooking. Do you really need a burger cooker that produces two burgers at a time? Your frying pan or broiler could do that. Do you have a popcorn popper stealing counter or cupboard space? I bet you could make A-1 popcorn in a Dutch oven. How about that deep-fat fryer that fries just enough for one or two or four? If you fry a lot, use a big one; if you just want to plop in an occasional doughnut or potato skin, what's wrong with a frying pan and a little oil?

We're all such suckers for advertising unless we understand that the primary purpose of a clever ad campaign is first to create a need and then to sell a product to meet that need. You're a big girl now; don't let advertising dictate your needs. Resist products you can't justify. Just because something's *new, new, new,* you're not required to give it house room.

To deal with the mess you already have, I recommend that you ruthlessly eliminate from your inventory any product, equipment, or appliance that you haven't used for two years (or less, if you're comfortable with a shorter time span). Store separately, out of the way, any items you use seasonally or objects of particular sentimental value. Proceed slowly, one room at a time; parting can be painful—particularly if you calculate the dollar value of all that junk. Have a garage sale to recoup some of your investment. Or just wave goodbye to the Salvation Army truck as it removes your checkered, untidy, disorganized past—and starts you on the road to systematic tranquillity.

Q. I don't have so many things, but the things I do need are never in the right place at the right time. How do I get organized?

A. The principle of organization I find most helpful is to store objects, as much as possible, at the point of first use. This simple rule helps put the items you want where you want them when you want them.

Take cereal bowls, for instance. I always kept mine with the rest of the dishes until I saw how silly it was to grab a bowl, dance across the kitchen for the cereal, tote it back to the bowl, pour it, and retrace my steps. Bowls and cereal are now stowed in the same cabinet. What silly rule says I can't break up a set of dishes?

Then there was the nail polish epiphany. My nail polish was always carefully ensconced on my dressing table because that's where ladies keep their cosmetics and beauty products, right? Wrong, if like me, they never sit at a dressing table long enough for a full manicure. I do my nails when I'm bushed, my mind's on hold, or I'm watching "Dallas." Now all the nail products are in a basket in front of the TV.

There are literally hundreds of small, daily routines like these that you'd probably alter if you ever thought about them. Reassess how you do your tasks and then reassign tools and utensils to convenient places. Your house or office may end up a little unorthodox, but you'll have space that works *for* you, not against you.

EXERCISE 19:

ONLY A COUPLE MORE DAYS FOR YOUR LOG!

DAY 20

Hard Questions

Today's the day for miscellaneous comments and questions—
those that can't be pigeonholed into tidy categories.

Q. Task stripping is stupid! When I was doing mine, I decided
that cooking should be moved out of the wife and mother
categories and into the home manager's column. Guess
what? I'm still cooking. It was all an exercise in futility. I
didn't accomplish a thing!

A. Yes, you did, You clarified your concepts regarding the roles
of wife and mother. Now you need to determine what it is a
home manager does.

One of the definitions of a manager is that he or she
achieves desired results through the allocation of resources,
one of which is people. A manager coordinates, plans, and
oversees; she doesn't carry out every detail herself.

For you, this may mean that it's time to fire up Dad and
the kids and begin to plan, coordinate, and oversee their

efforts in the kitchen. Or maybe you can find a Vo-Ed restaurant science student who'd like to use your kitchen as a lab. Search out a catering service that provides dinners to the families of busy women—for a price. Let your mind wander through the possibilities.

When you've investigated your choices, you may find that you'll have to keep right on stewing and sautéing. No management system guarantees to relieve you of all arduous labor; it only promises to assist you in your search for alternatives. Task stripping is a springboard to innovation, not an end in itself.

Q. I have a problem straightening out my priorities. I want to do a lot of things, all very important to me, but it seems that so many urgent needs arise to block my progress. My daughter needs two dozen cookies for Blue Birds *tomorrow*. My husband's ripped his best pair of pants. The dog's throwing up and has to go to the vet *now*. My life is constant petty problems—all someone else's. Where do I find the time for what's important to me?

A. You've put your finger on a very important distinction. A task that advances a goal or objective is important. A job that has to be done right now is urgent. Urgent tasks are sometimes important as well, but often they're just immediate.

Your Mission Statement should help you sort out urgencies from things that are important. If you eliminate certain nonessential functions from your area of concern, the emergencies that accompany those functions disappear as well.

All of which leaves you with what we might call unavoidable urgencies. A careful daily to-do list, with time built in for pop-up emergencies, can help stem your energy drain. Of course you can't predict when urgencies will arise, but if your schedule provides some unstructured time, you won't be thrown off course every time an emergency crops up. A flexible schedule can be shifted to accommodate the crisis without losing the day's momentum. I've had countless harrowing demonstrations that what I'm advocating here really works. Try it!

Q. Plan, plan, plan. Plan for jobs, plan for emergencies, plan for everything! Isn't there any room in your method for spontaneity?

A. Lots of people have the impression that planning prevents spontaneity. Lots of people are wrong. Women who plan the essentials in their lives are actually freer than those who run around all day being spontaneous. Having all your important ducks in a row liberates you from worry—and it's those niggling worries more than any other factor that inhibit extemporaneous fun.

Rigid schedules, hundred-item to-do lists, and clock watching indeed militate against impromptu pleasures, but if you've read this far you know that I'm calling for flexible schedules, short lists, and a lack of concern for conventional hours. In short, I'm calling for spontaneity.

Q. In one of the chapters you talk about sending strong "I-messages." What is an "I-message?"

A. For the answer to your question, I refer you to Linda Adams, author of *Effectiveness Training for Women.* She defines an "I-message" as "a statement that describes you . . . an expression of *your* feelings and experience." Such statements "do not contain evaluations, judgments, or interpretations of others."

I think "I-messages" can be very useful in engaging cooperation and creating good will. The major problem with them is that they seem to presuppose a particular response on the part of the receiver, and often that response just doesn't happen. Usually, at that point, I get very directive (e.g., "Get that coat off the floor!" as opposed to "I can't stand to see coats thrown all over the family room").

Even with this drawback, though, a home or office in which "I-messages" are the order of the day is a far pleasanter place than the same home or office in which every action is judged and evaluated—usually in critical tones.

Q. Don't you think that a lot of time management is tied to developmental stages? It's certainly easier to manage your own time when your kids are eighteen rather than eight—or eight months.

A. Yes, I do believe that we manage better at some periods of our lives than at others.

All of life is choosing. Choices mean consequences, and consequences can make for tough sledding at fairly predictable intervals.

The decision to marry brings with it the necessity to weigh another's feelings before taking substantial actions. The decision to have children means that pick-up-and-go freedom is curtailed in deference to the children's needs. The decision to go to work closes off picket-fence-and-apron fantasies. Choosing means you can't have it all—at least not all at once. I know that statement flies in the face of current feminist thinking, but I don't think having it all has anything to do with feminism. No man I know has it all either. Those single-mindedly scrambling up the ladder miss out on warmth and companionship even when it's offered to them. Men deeply involved in their families will end up making choices that will cost them money and/or advancement.

If we're blessed with our threescore and ten years, we might be fortunate enough to accomplish most of what we want to do with our lives, but I don't believe that at any one stage we can be equally good mothers, wives, employees (or employers), volunteers, and friends. We have to select which

priorities are of highest value at a particular point and concentrate our efforts on them. Flailing around, trying to make
every dream come true, right now, is a useless dissipation of
time.

Effective time management includes the ability to wait,
with patience, for the tide to turn. It will.

Even taking all this into account, though, I think that
good time management principles are applicable to every
stage of life. Women simply cannot put their lives on ice
while they wait for everyone else's developmental stages to
pass.

Q. I've been concerned throughout this book with your emphasis on self. You allude to the fact that service to others is
good, but then you weasel out by saying that women do too
much of it. What do you really mean?

A. I really mean that service to others is good, and that women
do too much of it.

To clarify all that, let's first define our terms. Service,
according to the *Reader's Digest Great Encyclopedic Dictionary,* is "assistance or benefit afforded another." I'm for
that. Servitude, on the other hand, is "enforced service (as
punishment for a crime)." I'm against that, and I believe that
too many women who think they're serving others are in fact
in servitude. The woman held hostage by her friend's expectations, the forty-year-old wife who asks her husband's permission to buy a new dress—and bakes him a cake when he
says yes; the mother who is everything and does everything
for her kids because *her* mother says she should—all are
trapped, enmeshed in a kind of emotional servitude.

Such women may spend their lives doing nice things for
people, but only because they believe they have no choice.
They sense their own existence in the positive regard of those
they cater to. Without that approbation, their identities are
incomplete. If you doubt the accuracy of that statement,

watch how inappropriately angry a servile woman becomes when the recipient of a good deed isn't sufficiently "grateful."

Service, however, is not simply doing good deeds to evoke a self-validating response. Service is a way of life that proceeds from real self-knowledge and awareness, and a desire to share with others one's talents, capabilities, and joy in life.

Service is bold, not cringing. It's positive, not apologetic. Service is generous, not calculating. It's risk taking, not safe. Service enriches a woman's life, rather than making her resentful. Service looks at a sink full of dishes and thanks God for food; servitude sees only the grease.

My concern with self, as you put it, is only to help women become aware of the distinction, and to realize that they have the power within them to change their lives and attitudes.

That's *my* service, and I think it's a good one, because as far as I'm concerned, though there can never be too many female servants, one female slave is more than enough.

EXERCISE 20:

"I THINK I CAN, I THINK I CAN"—MAINTAIN THE TIME LOG ONE MORE DAY!

DAY 21:

The Last Gasp and a New Start

You've made it! You've completed the program, and your most recent time logs are a graphic depiction of what's happened to you on this three-week odyssey. As your guide, let me be the first to congratulate you on sticking with what I know sometimes must have seemed like an endless, detail-ridden trek.

Now, don't blow it. Don't become complacent because you've been through the process once and your life is "organized." Don't fall prey to homeostasis. Homeostasis is a four-dollar scientific term that means that any system that has been altered tends to return to its original state. You've worked too hard to have that happen. Be on the lookout for backsliding and self-sabotage. Realize that life change is a fluid, continuous process. Unlike a cake or a roast or this book, you'll never be "done."

But at the same time, maintain your perspective. Remember that the system is for you, not you for the system. Don't get so tied up in goals and plans and efficiency and effectiveness that you can't laugh when it all falls apart, which occasionally will happen.

To illustrate how that can happen, here's a story, courtesy of my husband's attorney:

It was raining, and a young mother was trapped in the house with three crabby, sniffling little kids. In desperation, she called her mother-in-law. Their conversation follows:

YM: Oh, mother-in-law, I'm frantic. The library building committee is meeting here tonight. I can't send the kids out to play so I can clean, I can't get the dessert made because I'm out of sugar, and my hair needs washing. I'm a mess.

ML: Now, dear, relax, I'll be over with my cleaning lady. I'll entertain the kids while she tidies up. I've got some pastry in the freezer; I'll bring that along. When we're all done cleaning, I'll bring the kids home with me so you can soak in a hot tub.

YM: Oh, thank you! I'm going to call Stan at the office right now to tell him what an angel mother he has!

ML: Stan? My son's name is George. Honey, I'm afraid you have the wrong mother.

YM: Does this mean you're not coming?

Sometimes she's not coming. Some days will still be disasters. But you can handle them. You know how. Go to it. You're on your own.

EXERCISE 21:

1 Compare your two sets of time logs. Look at what you've done. Examine how you've changed. Clarify where you want to go with what you've learned. Do it!

and

2 Use the Time Management Goal Sheet included as a guide to chart your progress.

Time Management Goal Sheet

Mission Statement: What is the essence of this role for me?

Goals: What do I want?

Objectives: What will I change, when, and how will I know I've been successful?

Plans: How will I do it?

Scheduling: How do I make the time?

_____

Suggested Reading

General:
Briggs, Dorothy Corkille. *Celebrate Yourself.* Garden City, New York: Doubleday and Co., 1977.

Burns, David. *Feeling Good.* New York: William Morrow & Co., 1980.

DeRosis, Helen (with Victoria Y. Pellegrino). *The Book of Hope.* New York: Macmillan, 1976.

Dowling, Colette. *The Cinderella Complex.* New York: Summit Books, 1981.

Dyer, Wayne. *Pulling Your Own Strings.* New York: Thomas Y. Crowell Co., 1978.

Rubin, Theodore Isaac. *Compassion and Self-Hate.* New York: David McKay Co., 1975.

Scarf, Maggie. *Unfinished Business: Pressure Points in the Lives of Women.* Garden City, New York: Doubleday & Co., 1980.

Trahey, Jane. *On Women and Power: Who's Got It, How to Get It.* New York: Rawson Associates Publishers, Inc., 1977.

Management Issues:
Drucker, Peter. *The Effective Executive.* New York: Harper and Row, 1966–67.

————. *Managing for Results*. New York: Harper and Row, 1964.

Eisen, Carol. *Nobody Said You Had to Eat Off the Floor . . . The Psychiatrist's Wife's Guide to Housekeeping*. New York: David McKay Co., 1971.

Harragan, Betty Lehan. *Games Mother Never Taught You: Corporate Gamesmanship For Women*. New York: Rawson, Wade Publishers, Inc., 1977.

Henning, Margaret and Jardim, Anne. *The Managerial Woman*. Garden City, New York: Anchor Press/Doubleday, 1976–77.

Pogrebin, Letty Cottin. *Getting Yours*. New York: David McKay Co., 1975.

Sher, Barbara (with Annie Gottlieb). *Wishcraft*. New York: Viking Press, 1979.

Tennov, Dorothy. *Super Self*. New York: Funk & Wagnalls, 1977.

Winston, Stephanie. *Getting Organized*. New York: W. W. Norton & Co., 1978.

Time Management:

Bliss, Edwin. *Getting Things Done: The ABCs of Time Management*. New York: Charles Scribner's Sons, 1976.

Lakein, Alan. *How to Get Control of Your Time and Your Life*. New York: David McKay Co., 1973.

McKenzie, Alec and Waldo; Kay Cronkite. *About Time: A Woman's Guide to Time Management*. New York: McGraw-Hill Book Co., 1981.

Scott, Dru. *How to Put More Time in Your Life*. New York: Rawson, Wade Publishers, Inc., 1980.

Index

About Time (Mackenzie and Waldo), 67
Activists, and frazzle, 53–54, 86–91
Activities
doing two at once, 101–102
on time log, recording of, 12–13
Adams, Linda, 130
Anger, and depression, 84
Appointments
on daily to-do list, 74
scheduling, 63, 97
Attention getting, and procrastination, 75, 116
Authority, and delegation, 68, 69, 70, 110

Baby-step technique, for procrastination, 76, 77–78
Barter, 107–108
Beneficiary
and low level of satisfaction, 25

oneself as, 25–27
in task inventory, 17–18
Bliss, Edwin C., 100
Boredom, 75, 118–119
Bryant, Anita, 6
Burns, David, 84

Children
activities of, 97–98
appealing to sense of justice of, 105
choosing not to have, 7
continual driving of, 97–98
and delegation, 103–107
interruptions by, 62–63
of mother at home, 7
telephone answering by, 59
of working mother, 7
Choices, life
guilt about making, 7
standards governing, 6–8
"Cinderella Complex," 6
Clothing money, and Pareto Principle, 113

Commitment, full, 86, 87–88
Communication
  assertive, 31
  and cooperation, 70
  and delegation, 70
  "I-message," 31, 130–131
  about role change, 30–31
Compromises
  and role change, 32
  and value collisions, 111–112
Concentration, total, 64–65,
  101, 102
Consultation, about role
  change, 32
Convincing others, about role
  change, 31–32
Cooperation
  and communication, 70
  promoting, and role change,
  30–32
Culture, and women's roles, 26

Deadlines, 117
Delegation, 52–53, 67–71, 103–
  110
  and authority, 68, 69, 70, 110
  benefits of, 67
  and children, 103–107
  and Dumpers, 68–69
  and emphasis on results, 104
  and failure of person
    delegated, 109
  and fear of failure, 67
  and fear of relinquishing
    power, 68
  and fear of success, 68, 110
  and husbands, 108–109
  and managers, 70
  and perfectionism, 68
  and Saints, 69
  and strike tactic, 106–107
  and style, 70, 103–104, 110

on Time Log Analysis Sheet,
  54
Depression
  and anger, 84
  boredom as mask for, 119
  and fatigue, 83–85, 119
  professional intervention for,
  84–85
Discipline, 102
Dowling, Colette, 6
Drucker, Peter, 9, 35
Dumpers, and delegation, 68–
  69
Dyer, Wayne, 117

Effective Executive, The
  (Drucker), 9, 35
Effectiveness versus efficiency,
  34–35
*Effectiveness Training for
  Women* (Adams), 130
Efficiency, 102
  versus effectiveness, 34–35
Energy periods, high and low,
  82–83, 119–120, 122
  matching to job, 83, 85
  on time log, 13
Equipment
  failure of, 61
  preventive maintenance for,
  61
Excitement
  positive, engendering, 115
  and procrastination, 75, 114–
  115
Executive(s)
  definition of, 9
  effective, 28
  ineffective, 28
Executive mind-set, 28
Exercise, need for, 82

Failure, fear of and avoidance of
  delegation, 67
  and procrastination, 75–76
Fatigue, 53, 80–85, 118–122
  and boredom, 118–119
  depression causing, 83–84
  and energy periods, high and
    low, 82–83, 85, 119–120,
    122
  and exercise, need for, 82
  and filling in, 53
  overwork causing, 80–82
  and rest, needed for, 81–82
  and sleep pattern, 80–81
  on Time Log Analysis Sheet,
    55
  and work schedules, 119–120,
    121
Feeling Good (Burns), 84
Feelings, on time log, 13–14
Feminists, 6
Filling in, 111–117
  as inappropriate daily
    behavior, 53
  as sensible alternative when
    tired, 53
  on Time Log Analysis Sheet,
    54
  and values collisions, 111–112
Flextime, 119, 121
Flow chart, 47
Fonda, Jane, 6
Food money, and Pareto
  Principle, 113
Frazzle, 53–54, 86–91, 123–127
  and objects, 135–136
  overcommitment resulting
    in, 86–87, 123–124
  on Time Log Analysis Sheet,
    55
Friends
  helping, 95–96
  and housecleaning team, 107

Fritters, 52, 58–66, 95–102
  meditation for, 65, 102
  people-caused, 61–64, 95–99
  self-induced, 52, 63–65
  thing-caused, 58–61, 99–101
  on Time Log Analysis Sheet,
    54, 66
Fugue behavior
  definition of, 52
  and total concentration, 64–
    65

Getting Things Done (Bliss), 100
Gilbreth, Frank Bunker, 25
Goal(s)
  altering, 42
  and planning, 44. *See also*
    Planning
  setting, 35, 39, 40
  working together with
    objectives, 40–41
Gottlieb, Annie, 47
Guilt
  and long daily list, 73
  and making choices, 7
  and uncompleted tasks, 36
  and use of time, 6, 8

Help
  and barter, 105–106
  giving, to friends, 95–96
  hiring, 108, 109
Home manager, 128–129
Homeostasis, 134
Housewife. *See also* Wife
  choosing role of, 7
*How to Get Control of Your
  Time and Your Life*
  (Lakein), 73
*How to Put More Time in Your
  Life* (Scott), 75
How to Meditate (LeShan), 65

Husbands. *See also* Men
  and delegation, 108–109
  of working wife, 7

"Ideal woman," 7–8, 9–10
"I-message" communication,
  31, 130–131
Inconveniences, 11–12, 129–130
Interruptions, 58. *See also*
  Fritters
Inventory
  of supplies, 60
  task. *See* Task inventory

Job sharing, 119–120
Justice, appealing to children's
  sense of, 105

Lakein, Alan, 73
LeShan, Lawrence, 65
Life changes, major, 27
Life choices, 6–8
List, daily to-do, 72, 73–74, 77,
  78–79
  and guilt, 73
  length of, 73, 113–114, 130
  need for, 114
  and objectives, 73–74
  time for emergencies in, 129
Little Way of St. Theresa, 65,
  102

Mackenzie, Alec, 67
Manager(s)
  definition of, 128
  and delegation, 70
  home, 128–129
Marriage, and choice, 7
Meditation, 65, 102

Meetings, unproductive, 98–99
Men. *See also* Husbands
  as role models, 108
  roles for, 26
  self-care for, 27
  time management by, 5
Mission Statement, 34, 37–38,
  42–43, 47–48, 129
Money
  clothing, 113
  food, 113
  and Pareto Principle, 112–113

Needs of others, responding to,
  7, 8, 9–10

Objective(s), 39–43
  activities enhancing, 89–90
  alteration of, 42
  criteria in choosing, 41–42
  on daily to-do list, 72–73
  elements of, 39
  and fritters, 52
  and planning, 44–48
  working together with goals,
    40–41
Objects
  and frazzle, 125–126
  mislaid, 60–61
  organization of, 125–127
  and Pareto's Principle, 126
Organization, of objects, 125–
  127
Organizations
  joining, as condition of
    employment, 124–125
  and overcommitment and full
    commitment, 86–91,
    123–124
  resignation from, 91, 123–124

Overcommitment, frazzle
caused by, 86–87, 123–124
Overwork, fatigue caused by,
80–82

Pareto, Vilfredo, 112
Pareto Principle, 73, 111
and money, 112–113
and objects, 126
Parent, single, 107, 121
Parkinson's Law, 8–9
Perfectionism
and avoidance of delegation,
68
circumventing, 102
Planning, 44–48, 114
alternate, 46–47
backward, 45–47
and spontaneity, 130
Power, fear of relinquishing,
and avoidance of
delegation, 68
Priorities
assessment of, 13
and filling in, 53
and life stages, 132
living in tune with, 11–12
on time log, 13
on Time Log Analysis Sheet,
54
Procrastination, 53, 72–79, 114–
117
as attention getter, 75, 116
and boredom, 75
conscious, 74–75
and deadline setting, 117
and denial of satisfaction, 77
and excitement, 75, 114–115
and fear of failure, 75–76
and fear of success, 76–77
and planning, 46

professional intervention for,
77
and task termination, 115–116
unconscious, 75–77
Professional intervention
for depression, 84–85
for procrastination, 77

*Reader's Digest Great Encyclo-
pedic Dictionary*, 132
Resignations, from
organizations, 91, 123–124
Rest, need for, 81–82
Results, desired, 24–25, 28–29
Role(s)
and culture, 26
in task inventory, 16, 17, 18
tasks in essential core of, 37–
38
Role change, 27–29
and communication, 30–31
and compromising, 32
and convincing others, 31–32
and consultation with others,
32
others affected by, 30–33
and promotion of
cooperation, 30–32
Role confusion, 16, 37
Role model(s)
male, 108
and standards governing life
choices, 6
Routine, overhauling, 120–121
Routine tasks, 25

St. Theresa's Little Way, 65,
102
Saints, and delegation, 69
Satisfaction, denial of, and
procrastination, 77

Satisfaction level
  low, and beneficiaries, 25
  low, and roles, 28
  in task inventory, 17, 18
Scarf, Maggie, 84
Schlafly, Phyllis, 6
Scott, Dru, 75
Self, concern with, 89–90, 132–133
Self-care, 25–27
Self-hatred, 116
Self-image, and procrastination, 77
Service
  definition of, 132
  to others, 7, 8, 9–10, 132–133
  versus servitude, 132, 133
Servitude versus service, 132, 133
Sher, Barbara, 47
Sleep patterns, 80–81
Spontaneity, and planning, 130
Strike tactic, 106–107
Success, fear of
  and avoidance of delegation, 68, 110
  and procrastination, 76–77
Super Self (Tennov), 52
Supplies
  needed for tasks, 60–61
  organizing, 127

Task(s)
  in essential core of role, 37–38
  routine, 25
  supplies needed for, 60–61
  uncompleted, and guilt, 36
Task inventory, 16–23, 25, 26, 28, 74
Task stripping, 37, 112, 128, 129

Task termination, pain of, 115–116
Telephone
  as avoidance mechanism, 63–64
  and call-ending strategies, 98–100
  and call-waiting, 100–101
  excessive outgoing calls on, 63–64
  management strategies for, 58–60, 99–101
Telephone answering machine, 59
Telephone hours, scheduled, 59–60, 101
Tennov, Dorothy, 52
Thomas, Marlo, 6
Time
  in task inventory, 17, 18
  on time log, 13
Time log, 11–15
  maintaining, 12, 14, 16, 18, 24, 29, 33, 38, 43, 48, 85, 95, 102, 110, 117, 122, 127, 133, 136
  sample, 15
Time Log Analysis Sheet, 54–56, 66
  sample, 57
Time management
  by men, 5
  traditional approach to, 8–9
Time Management Goal Sheet, 136
Time mismanagement. *See also specific area*
  major areas of, 51–56
Timers, 64

Unfinished Business (Scarf), 84
Unworthiness, 77

Urgent tasks, 11–12, 129–130

Value structure, 11, 38
  and conflict, 12
Values collisions, 111–112
Visiting, and fritters, 64

Waldo, Kay Cronkite, 67
Wife. *See also* Housewife
  good, task-oriented definition
    of, 35–36
Wishcraft (Sher and Gottlieb),
  47
Women

as beneficiaries of own
    actions, 25–27
  ideal, 7–8, 9–10
  working, 7
Women's barter network, 107
Women's movement, 26, 27
Work ethic, 120
Work schedules, 119–120, 121
Working
  and children, 7
  as choice, 7
  and husband, 7

Your Erroneous Zones
  (Dyer), 117